My Creator, My Friend

ALSO BY BRUCE LARSON

Wind and Fire
Luke, Communicator's Commentary, vol. 3
There's a Lot More to Health Than Not Being Sick
Risky Christianity
The Whole Christian
No Longer Strangers
The One and Only You
Ask Me to Dance
The Emerging Church
Dare to Live Now
Thirty Days to a New You
Setting Men Free
Living on the Growing Edge
Believe and Belong

WITH KEITH MILLER:

The Edge of Adventure
Living the Adventure
The Passionate People: Carriers of the Spirit

My Creator, My Friend

The Genesis of a Relationship

Bruce Larson

WORD BOOKS
PUBLISHER
WACO, TEXAS

A DIVISION OF
WORD, INCORPORATED

67898 BKC 987654321

Unless otherwise noted, all Scripture quotations are from the Revised
Standard Version, copyright 1946 (renewed 1973), 1956, and © 1971
by the Division of Christian Education of the National Council of Churches
of Christ in the USA, and are used by permission.

Library of Congress Cataloging-in-Publication Data

Larson, Bruce.
  My creator, my friend.

  1. Bible. O.T. Genesis—Criticism, interpretation,
etc. I. Title.
BS1235.2.L33 1986   222'.1106   85-22794
ISBN 0-8499-0458-7

Printed in the United States of America

Dedicated to
those who have yet to discover
that God is their Friend

Contents

Foreword

Few things have changed my life as much as writing this particular book. It is as though God drew back a curtain and showed me a landscape that I did not dream existed and let me step into that landscape.

When I became a Christian many years ago, it was because I met the Person of Jesus Christ. Who would not be overwhelmed by His love, humility and gentleness and grace? Later I became more keenly aware of the Holy Spirit in all of His mysterious and intimate peace and power. But the third member of the Trinity, God, Father and Creator, seemed distant and inaccessible. Even though I read and studied the Old Testament faithfully, I think I was somewhat afraid of the God portrayed there. Madelyn Murray O'Hair claims that a serious reading of the Old Testament while still a teenager turned her from Presbyterianism to atheism, for which she has become our nation's leading champion.

At any rate, this book was born when I decided to research the book of Genesis, to examine thoroughly the God revealed there, and then preached my observations and conclusions to my beloved and faithful family at University Presbyterian Church in Seattle. It was an astonishing experience. I now know that the face of God revealed in the book of Genesis is the same one that I see when I look into the face of Jesus. Jesus said, "He who has seen me has seen the Father. . . . I and the Father am one" (John 14:9, 10:30). I have come to understand anew the truth of that astonishing declaration. Genesis underscores again and again that friendship is the key to our relationship with the Father. Jesus said to His disciples, "No longer do I call you servants . . . but I have called you friends . . ." (John 15:15). James says, "Abraham believed God and it was reckoned to him as righteousness, and he was called a friend of God" (James 2:23).

We read in the Gospels that Jesus forgave His doubting and vacillating disciples and called them His friends, and that is entirely consistent with His nature. In Genesis God the Creator continues to love and pursue His chosen people and desires their friendship, in spite of their failures and betrayals. From the biblical perspective, righteousness is not certainty about my own faith or obedience or purity. Righteousness is believing in a God who is loving and powerful enough to lead me, if only I trust Him. To believe and trust in God rather than ourselves is to become His friend. That's the clear message of Genesis.

On days when life is difficult and I feel overwhelmed, as I do fairly often, it helps to remember in my prayers that all God requires of me that day is to trust Him and be His friend. I find I can do that.

My hope is that others, in reading this book, will find that the God of Genesis is their Friend.

Finally, credit where credit is due. Feedback from my loyal family in Christ at University Presbyterian Church in Seattle was invaluable, for each of these chapters was first a sermon. But even more crucial was the editing by my wife and best friend, Hazel. It is a long sea-mile between a bunch of sermons, no matter how well received, and a book. There would be no book apart from Hazel. All credit to her skill and patience. Thanks also to my friend Ernie Owen, Editorial Director at Word, for believing in this book from the start, and to his colleague and my long-time friend Pat Wienandt, for her careful polishing and correcting. Finally, for their typing after hours, their encouragement, and, most of all, their love and friendship, I want to thank my colleagues Gretha Osterberg and Hal Jaenson.

My
Creator,
My
Friend

1. How It All Began

Genesis 1:1–2:3

A good many Christians confess to having difficulty with the God of the Old Testament. Their impression is that He is a stern, demanding, sometimes vengeful God—a very different God than the one revealed in the Gospels in the person of Jesus Christ or in the book of Acts in the presence of the Holy Spirit.

I was conscious of these concerns as I undertook this study of Genesis, a book so ancient that parts of it are considered prehistoric. The God I found there is revealed, first of all, as the Creator of the Universe and all that is in it, including the human race. It seems just as clear that the purpose of it all was to create beings with whom He could enter into a relationship, a relationship of love and friendship. I remain convinced that the God of the New Testament, incarnate in the person of Jesus, is exactly the same God we read about in Genesis.

We should not be surprised. Jesus says, "He who has seen me has seen the Father; . . . I and the Father are one" (John 14:9; 10:30). Certainly Genesis is peopled with strange characters—funny, old Hebrew types and even pre-Hebrew types—and their customs are difficult to understand and identify with. But the God who is acting and revealing Himself throughout this ancient story is the same God who is acting and revealing Himself throughout the New Testament and in and through His people today.

It seems to me that Genesis is a gold mine of basic theology and particularly of applied theology. Let's keep in mind that all of us are theologians. Princeton Theological Seminary president Dr. Thomas Gillespie has said, "Theology is how we integrate the truth we believe about God into the lives we live." That means that all of us who are believers are also theologians. As we read our Bibles, as we pray or worship, individually or corporately, we ought to be asking God what all this means for our jobs, our marriages, our relationships, all that we do.

For all of us, then, who are theologians, this first Old Testament book is crucial. Of all the Old Testament books, none is closer in subject matter, content, and revelation to the books of the New Testament. That does not mean that Genesis does not present some problems. We find, for example, at least two creation stories, similar yet different. But in spite of those problems, Genesis provides many lighthouses along the way where the beam shines forth unmistakably and we can't miss its illuminating light. In the next chapters we'll be zeroing in on those portions of Genesis where God reveals some of those pivotal truths about who He is and who we are.

To begin with, let's bear in mind that Genesis is not a scientific book. It is broader than that. It was not intended to be a geological or astronomical treatise of how the world began. Nevertheless, when *Time* magazine did a feature on cosmology a few years ago, here's what the article said: "Most cosmologists, scientists who study the structure and evolution of the universe, agree that the biblical account of creation in imagining an initial void may be uncannily close to the truth. The universe, they believe, is the expanding remnant of a huge fireball that was created 20 million years ago by the explosion of a giant primordial atom." We are left with the conclusion that before science existed, God revealed some truths about the universe to a group of people living in prehistoric times. Those stories were passed along orally until the time of Moses, who, according to tradition, gathered together those accounts and wrote the first five books of the Bible, called the Pentateuch. It seems clear that before science existed an ancient race of people had an understanding of the creation by means of divine revelation.

In my seminary days at Princeton, Albert Einstein was my neighbor. He lived just three houses from my dormitory. This great scientist once confessed that science did not provide him with the language he needed to do his advanced thinking, and that he was compelled to use theological language. He seems to be saying that theology predates and is the groundwork for science. When science exhausts itself, we are left with theology. In studying Genesis, or indeed any book of the Bible, I think we need to be looking most of all for God's self-revelation.

Recently, my denomination constructed some guidelines for studying the Bible that I think are particularly helpful. I'll share just the first three because they will serve as our guidelines in the coming chapters.

1. Recognize the centrality of God's self-revelation in Jesus Christ as the heart of biblical witness. (That central revelation is the whole purpose of the Bible. God begins to reveal Himself first of all in Genesis and ultimately in the Gospels through Jesus Christ.)

2. Focus on the plain text of Scripture in its grammatical and historical context, rather than allegory and subjective fantasy. (Preachers and laypeople alike love to dwell on all the hidden meanings in Scripture. Instead of wondering about obscure meanings, why not take the Bible at its word? God has revealed what He really means.)

3. Depend upon the guidance of the Holy Spirit in interpreting and applying God's message. (I hope you'll be doing just that as we explore together the book of Genesis in these next chapters.)

The Nature of God

One of the first things we learn in Genesis is that God is a personal God. He's not a force—not a big bang. He might have caused the big bang, but He Himself is a person. Creation was accomplished in six days, according to chapter one, and on the seventh, God rested. We deduce from that that He is a person or personality. He works and He rests and He observes the rhythm of life. In verse 26 we find God saying, "Let us make man in our image." Here is the first glimpse of the concept of the triune God. John begins his Gospel by speaking of Jesus as the Word. In verses 2 and 3 he says, "He was in the beginning with God; all things were made through Him, and without Him was not anything made that was made." From the beginning Jesus existed with the Father and the Holy Spirit: one God, three persons. The Messiah, the anointed one, the Christ, preexisted and was co-Creator of the universe.

Genesis, then, begins with the proposition that God is and that He is the prime mover who created the universe. In all the subsequent chapters we find the interweaving of the two great themes of Genesis—law and grace. God has given us law, laws about our life together. If we break those laws, there are consequences. We damage ourselves and injure others. God is a God of order, and it is in our own best interests to follow His laws. But the God revealed in Genesis, as through the whole New Testament, is also a God of grace. If we break His laws, consciously or unconsciously, He suffers with us. He is there saying, "I love you. I want to help you." His absolute laws do not change, but His grace is available in our failure.

A friend of mine told me about a conversation she had overheard in a doctor's waiting room. A little four-year-old came in with his mother, and during the seemingly interminable wait to see the doctor, this little boy kept up a steady stream of questions, ranging from "Where is the doctor and why are we here?" to more theological subjects like "Who is God and why isn't He married?" Finally the little boy asked what seemed the ultimate question. "Mom, why doesn't God ever just get tired and stop?" The mother thought for a minute before she replied, "Because God is love and love never gets tired." This young woman was modeling just the kind of patience God has with us. He doesn't say, "You dummy, you did it again." He loves us, and His grace is always operating. All through Genesis we find God's grace superseding His laws.

Our Story

The truth of Genesis is confirmed for me because I find it is my story, just as it's your story. I am Adam, I am Cain, I am Abel. I am Abraham and Isaac and Jacob. I am Sarah and Rachel and Rebekah. Their stories are my stories. Let's suppose for a moment that some friend or neighbor or even an editor asked you to write your story. How would you do that? Would you list all the grades you received through your school years or catalogue all your possessions, the things you have collected over the years which are displayed in your home or stored in your attic? Your grades and your belongings are a very small part of who you are. You might come up with a chronology: "I had the flu when I was seven, I went to camp at ten, I had my tonsils out at thirteen," etc. However, my guess is that in order to write any mean-ingful autobiography, as some of you will some day, you would try to recapture some significant stories, those things that happened to you that capsulize relationships and emo-tions you experienced at age seven or nine or fourteen. Those stories become the means of understanding your uniqueness. In Genesis, God has given us this kind of story. The people and events recorded here give us glimpses of the Creator.

Who and Why

For me, the very first verse in Genesis is one of the two great tentpoles of the faith, the other being John 3:16. These verses seem to summarize all we know about God and life. Genesis answers the *who* of life: "In the beginning *God* created the heavens and the earth." John 3:16 answers the *why*. "God so loved the world [His creation] that he gave his only begotten Son, that whosoever believeth in him should not perish, but have everlasting life" (KJV). On the who and the why of those two verses we could hang the whole tapestry of theology. That beginning verse of Genesis establishes the fact that we are not set adrift in some mindless universe. God is the Creator of it all and our Father. The verse in John's Gospel capsulized that which was in the mind of God from the beginning—the incarnation, our redemption, and the gift of eternal life.

Genesis 1:1 is a pivotal verse. *God is.* It ought to be apparent that behind creation there is a Creator. We see a house and assume there was an architect. We examine a watch and know a watchmaker conceived of it and designed it. We read a poem and are aware that somewhere, sometime, a poet created those words. Scientists presently studying the human brain say they have no idea how it works. It's in a whole different league from a computer. It's like a million computers or microchips. The capacities of the human brain are beyond comprehension, and even scientists are beginning to suspect there's a "who" behind the brain.

Here's what a dermatologist wrote about our skin: "In one square inch of skin you will find 20 blood vessels; 65 hairs and muscles; 78 nerves; 78 sensors for heat, 13 for cold, 165 for pressure; 100 sebaceous glands; 650 sweat glands; 1300 nerve endings; and nineteen million, five hundred thousand cells." We might well ask what mind conceived of skin.

The hand of the Creator seems so apparent; yet it goes

unrecognized by so many. We Calvinists would say that our blindness is largely a matter of sin, which clouds the horizon and hampers our vision. I once spent three days in Illinois at a conference with Jonas Salk, the gifted scientist. When asked about his optimism, he said, "I see the same blackness, hear the same thunder, see the same lightning everyone else does. But I ascribe this not to the end, but to the beginning. I see the dangers we face now as a possibility for human beings to evolve to a new stage; to respond consciously to the threats of our survival; to do something about our survival and not leave it entirely to chance." Salk is a visionary instead of a doomsayer because he sees a new beginning while others see only more problems. When we understand from Genesis 1:1 that in the beginning *God is,* we have a lens for viewing all life, whether we are looking at the world outside or trying to see into ourselves.

In 1983, when Alexander Solzhenitsyn received the Templeton Award in London, he began his speech by saying, "Over half a century ago while I was still a child, I recall hearing a number of older people offer the following explanation for the great disasters that had befallen Russia; 'Men have forgotten God. That's why all this has happened.' . . . And if I were called upon to identify briefly the principal trait of the entire 20th Century, here, too, I would be unable to find anything more precise and pithy than to repeat once again, 'Men have forgotten God.' "*

Genesis 1:1 answers the questions of how and by whom all life began. The conviction that *God is* affects all that we are and do. Our personal and corporate destiny hinges on whether or not we believe God is the Creator. Even Benjamin Franklin, hardly known for his piety, said, "I have lived, sir, a long time, and the longer I live, the more convincing proof I see of this truth—that God governs in the affairs of men." Genesis gives you and me that first central truth that

---

* *The New Yorker,* May 30, 1983.

God is and that He is our Creator. If you (or I, or anyone else) are created, then you are not the result of some biological accident. You were planned by the Creator and you are important to Him. You have worth. You can't afford to fail deliberately. Your success or failure has new meaning and eternal consequences.

People have said to me, "Aren't you Christians arrogant? You think that with all that science has learned about the cosmos, that God cares about people on this little pimple of earth over here in the suburbs of the universe?" For the sake of argument, pretend for a moment that you are God. That means that you are at the center of the universe. The earth, on the other hand, would be a little flyspeck in a suitcase (that's our universe or solar system) sitting in some remote place like the Falkland Islands. What then, as God, is your relationship to this remote suburb of the cosmos, this tiny, insignificant Planet Earth?

First of all, keep in mind that scientists tell us we can stop worrying about UFOs from another planet—there will be none. Chances are all too remote of the right elements coming together on any other planet to support life anything like ours. If earth were one degree closer to the sun, we'd burn up. One degree farther away and we'd freeze. We're told that the odds are one trillion to one that a galaxy that has another planet like Earth exists. Very possibly, in this vast universe, we may be the only creatures who can know God and respond to His love. If life is discovered on some other planet, I'll be thrilled, but right now, it looks as if we're all alone in the universe.

The Bible begins by revealing that in the beginning God made all that is and created man to have a relationship with Him. A rabbi I know received a letter from a little girl in his Hebrew class, one she wrote after a lesson on the deliverance of the Israelites by the parting of the Red Sea. She writes, "Dear God: My teacher read us the part where all the Jews went through where the water was and got away.

Keep up the good work. I'm Jewish. Love, Paula." When we claim the truth revealed in Genesis, we can write, "Dear God: The Bible says that out of the whole universe, we're the reason for the creation. I can't believe it, but keep up the good work. I'm human." If we believe that in the beginning God *was* and *is* and *made* us, and that then in Christ He *redeemed* us, all of life changes. That's the point of orientation for living our lives personally and corporately now and forevermore.

Unchanging Landmarks

One summer while on vacation, my wife and I, along with our son and daughter-in-law, chartered a little sailboat in the San Juan Islands for a weekend. We decided to journey to the charming Canadian city of Victoria. At the end of the first day we found ourselves about two miles away from our destination. The wind was up, the sun was out, and the boat was heeled over with her sails full. The kelp and seaweed were swirling by at a fast clip. After two hours of this kind of glorious sailing, son Mark, who always grasps the situation quicker than his father, broke the unpleasant news. "We're going no place. That lighthouse is in the same place it was two hours ago." He was dead right. We were making great speed and going nowhere because powerful tidal currents had been working against us all the way.

Without a fixed point on the horizon, we can be moving through life at a fast pace and going nowhere. We can't know if we're making progress unless we've got some fixed benchmark outside the circumstances of our lives that reminds us who we are and who it is we are serving. The old Amish saying "The hurrieder I go, the behinder I get" is all too true if we do not have some fixed point from which to measure the progress we are or are not making.

We have, I think, just two choices. We worship either God or man. Either we believe that God is Creator or we

believe that the universe and everything in it is the result
of man's own efforts. I was amazed recently to read about
some entrepreneur who spent a half million dollars to buy
an assortment of Elvis Presley artifacts, including a one-
thousand-dollar pair of undershorts. He takes this collection
around the country, and in each major city at least 200,000
people pay money to see the Elvis Presley artifacts. A lot
of women and even some men go wild over this display.
Most of us are aware that Presley, in his last years, overate
himself into obesity. His drug abuse rendered him incompe-
tent much of the time. He watched porno movies non-stop.
Certainly he had an influence, probably a lasting one, on
the pop music of this century, but that hardly explains the
worship of this dead entertainer. The phenomenon seems
to say less about Elvis Presley than it does about us. But
without the benchmark of Genesis 1:1, "In the beginning
God . . ." who was and is, we need someone or something
to take God's place, and too often we make heroes of those
of dubious accomplishments and fleeting fame.

There was a tragic plane crash in our area recently when
a plane hit the mountains in a fog. A commercial pilot made
this comment to me, "It's tragic and unnecessary. Pilots are
taught to go up when they can't see in the fog. They keep
going up until they *can* see. That's a cardinal rule." It's not
a bad rule for your life and mine. Take time to look up
and tell God you're lost, in your business, marriage, career,
or your dating life. He can help you regain your perception
of reality and you may find your way back through the fog.

With Genesis 1:1 as my benchmark, I feel confident of
the sovereignty of God, even in the face of nuclear holocaust.
We have to work as though it all depends on us to avoid
such an eventuality, but, I confess to you that I don't think
the world will blow itself up until God ordains it. He may
do that through a Russian-U.S. confrontation. But God is
Creator, and we who are created cannot destroy His creation
without His assent.

Wallace Hamilton tells a poignant story about his four-year-old son. The family was staying at their summer home and little John was in a sulk. His mother and grandmother had gone off for a walk in the woods, leaving him behind. Wallace, who had been watching his son, saw him suddenly set off into the woods to find the two women. "I could have stopped him," said Wallace. "But I decided instead to follow him from a distance. John plodded for almost a mile before he gave up on finding his mother and grandmother. He became frightened and tired and began to cry. He turned as if to go back, but he didn't know which way to go. I stepped out of the bush by his side. 'Well, John,' I asked, 'are we going home?' John was not at all surprised to find his father. Giving me his hand, he solemnly said, 'John's lost.' "

When you find yourself lost this week or this month or this year, as you probably will, remember you were created by a friend who loves you and who has a plan for you. Hear Him say to you, "Put your hand in mine and let's go home."

2. How It All Went Wrong

Genesis 2:15–3:13

In 1921 the police in Philadelphia picked up a twenty-four-year-old woman who was wandering about and mumbling incoherently. They took her to a mental hospital where she remained for forty-eight years until someone discovered that she was speaking Ukrainian. At the time she was picked up, the young woman was in a dazed state because her husband and son had just died. But the tragedy is that no one realized she was speaking an existing language.

The Bible is God's own powerful, living, written word. But often we wander about in confusion because we don't know the language. A basic problem is that we who are products of the Western world have learned the language of the left hemisphere of the brain, a logical, cognitive, scientific, measurable way to communicate. We want the Bible to speak to us in those terms. But, when God chose the Israelites, He chose a "right-brain" people. (The right side of the brain is the intuitive, creative side.) His word comes to us through them and they are primarily a people who speak in a verb-dominated, action language. We Westerners tend to equate our left-brain kind of education with intelligence. My own college days only reinforced my conviction that lots of simpletons graduate from college. Education doesn't automatically make people wise. Basic reading and writing skills don't make you intelligent.

I have twice visited in the Rift Valley near Nairobi where Masai Christians gather around campfires in their villages at night to read the Bible. Perhaps only one member of the tribe can actually read and that person explains the scriptures for the others, but the spiritual wisdom that comes out of these illiterate people is extraordinary. We need to bring that kind of fresh understanding to the right-brain language of the Bible. Chapters 2 and 3 of Genesis reveal so much to us of who God is and what His mind is and what He intends for us to be and do. Let's explore some of these verses to see what they say in picture language.

Friendship Requirements

Let's call the first picture "Requirement for Friendship." Verses 15 through 17 say, "The Lord God took the man and put him in the Garden of Eden to till it and keep it. And the Lord commanded the man, saying, 'You may freely eat of every tree of the garden; but of the Tree of the Knowledge of Good and Evil you shall not eat, for in the day that you eat of it you shall die.' " From these verses we learn what God intends for us—to give us everything, food, abundance, a pleasant land, a pleasant climate, peace. He has created all of this for us and intends to be our friend but there is one law. There's one tree, the fruit of which Adam and Eve are not to eat. That was necessary.

The point is, that in any relationship of love, divine or human, there must be a boundary which tests a relationship. Suppose someone proposed marriage to you in this way: "I want to marry you, but I want a free and open relationship with no rules. I plan to do whatever I please in the years ahead." You'd say, "No way, Mac or Madame." The relationship of love requires some boundaries. We make commitments and promises. We say, "Because I love you I will never do certain things, or I will try to do and be certain other things." So it is with God. He said to Adam and Eve, "I love you. It's all yours. Just keep my law to prove that you trust me." That's the contract between man and God we find in picture one.

Meant for Relationship

Picture number 2 we'll call "Meant for Relationship." Beginning with verse 18 we read, "Then the Lord God said, 'It is not good that the man should be alone; I will make him a helper fit for him.' So out of the ground the Lord God formed every beast of the field and every bird of the air and brought them to the man to see what he would call them. And whatever the man called every living creature, that was its name." God made the animals for man's enjoyment and pleasure. Many Eastern cultures believe that to know something or someone's name gives you power over that person or thing. In picture form, we see man naming all the birds and beasts in creation, indicating that we are meant to have dominion over the world. We have to admire Adam's creativity as he moves through the whole bunch from aardvark to zebra. But after they were all named, God realized that none of those could be a helper fit for Adam.

These verses give us a pivotal view of the creation story. The animals did not prove to be a helper fit for Adam. He needed someone with whom he could have a relationship. What makes human beings unique? It is not merely our intelligence, for someday some animal may evolve that proves to be more intelligent than we. Animal lovers insist that animals have souls and I'm not about to argue with them. But pets cannot ultimately fulfill our need for relationships. We can pat our dog or throw him a ball or a stick, but he can have no real community with us on our level. We were made for relationship, with God, our Father, and with all the other children in His family. We are unique in all of creation, the Bible says, because God made us in His image and breathed into us His Spirit. Spirit and soul are not the same. When you die your spirit leaves you while your soul is redeemed. In His last words on the cross, Jesus said, "I offer up my spirit." The spirit is the very breath of God and because He has breathed His very life into us, we are unlike any other animal.

I believe in the creation story the Bible gives us. But even if I did not, if I believed we humans evolved from lower species, nevertheless, I would still conclude that at some point something drastic happened that separated man from the animals. One of the creatures in God's universe was given a new kind of life, the Spirit of God Himself. And that is not the result of evolution, it is a gift from our Creator. A process began by God's initiation that made us capable of entering into a relationship with Him.

Community

The title of picture number 3 is "Community." We find it in the concluding verses of chapter 2. God caused a deep sleep to fall upon the man and while he slept He took one of his ribs and made a woman and brought her to the man. Adam cried that at last this was bone of his bone and flesh of his flesh. She should be called woman. "Therefore a man leaves his father and his mother and cleaves to his wife, and they become one flesh. And the man and his wife were both naked and were not ashamed." In these verses we have a glimpse of the ideal human condition psychologically as well as theologically. God intended us to have community with one another, marriage, of course, being the most intimate human community possible. He caused Adam to sleep in order that the miracle might be accomplished.

Miracles still happen in our sleep. Occasionally God can resolve things in our unconscious mind that we can't resolve when we are awake. Since that first time Adam dozed off, sleep has been a great gift. When Adam awoke, he was missing a rib and we find that God has cloned a human being. It's beyond understanding how a human being could be constructed from a rib. And yet we know today that one cell in the body—one fingernail cell, one skin cell, one eye cell—could be cloned to reproduce you entirely. One cell contains all the necessary materials. God knew that long before scientists discovered it. He cloned Eve, a helpmate, and much more.

This past year one of our most renowned biblical scholars, David Freedman, a Presbyterian professor in Pittsburgh Seminary, published an article in *Biblical Archeology Review* about these verses. His findings indicate that "helpmate" is a mistranslation of the original words used in 2:18. The Hebrew is ᶜêzer-kᵉnegdô. In all of his research into the early Canaanite language, he found no evidence that ᶜêzer-kᵉnegdô means helpmate. Rather, it means a power "equal to" or "corresponding to him." God did not create any second-class human beings. The old Hebrew commentaries all confirm this—that women were co-existent and equal to men. Studies of the old language now confirm this conclusively. God did not make a helpmate. He made a second part of the same whole, somebody just like Adam who happened to be female.

In these beginning chapters of Genesis, we see God bestowing the gift of marriage, the ultimate human community. In a wedding, it used to be customary for the father to give the bride away. I think that might have had its beginnings here in Genesis. God is the father of the bride. He presents the bride to Adam. How much we need to be reminded that marriage and romance and love and sex are all good things authored by God. Until recently Christians have left the implications of that unexplored. Poets, playwrights, and novelists for centuries have romanticized love and marriage, and God is the instigator and Creator of it all.

My wife recently found a poem by Thomas More which moved her profoundly and which a friend has since printed in calligraphy and framed for her.

To keep one sacred flame through life unchilled, unmoved.
To love in wintery age the same as first in youth we loved.

To feel that we adore, even to fond excess
That though the heart would break with more, it could not
  live with less.

God created human beings capable of that kind of emotion. In this, our third right-brain picture, God is telling us that this is the way we are meant to live. Perhaps that explains why divorce is such a tragedy. It is not a matter of determining who is the guilty party and assigning blame. We all sin all the time. But in marriage, two people become one flesh, one soul, one being, and a new entity is born. When you divorce, that living organism is torn in two. You may survive that wound, but you never really recover from it.

The last verse in the chapter gives us a prescription for ideal marriage. "They were naked and not ashamed." What does it mean to be naked and not ashamed? Of course, they were at that time physically naked, that's obvious. But more than that, I think the implication is that they were psychologically naked. There were no hiding places, no secrets, no subterfuges, no game-playing. Each was totally known by the other. And with that kind of relationship, the sexual act becomes a sacramental, physical expression of a spiritual reality.

Marriage disintegrates as we begin to keep secrets from each other. The sexual act becomes a means to oneness, instead of an expression of it. When you begin to keep secrets in marriage, you become less and less spontaneous and marriage becomes routine or boring. God has made us for intimacy, beginning with Adam and Eve. They were unashamed. This whole matter of shame has puzzled psychologists for centuries. Why is it that humans feel shame and animals don't? We find the answer in Genesis. Shame is the result of keeping secrets, of hiding something.

Where It All Went Wrong

We will call picture number 4 "Where It All Went Wrong." The serpent tempted the woman to eat of the fruit of the Tree of Good and Evil.

The woman said to the serpent, "We may eat of the fruit of the trees of the garden, but God said, 'You shall not eat of the fruit of the tree in the midst of the garden, neither shall you touch it lest you die.' " The serpent said to the woman, "You will not die." [A barefaced lie.] "For God knows that when you eat of it your eyes will be opened, you will be like God knowing good and evil."

So when the woman saw that the tree was good for food and that it was a delight to the eye and the tree was to be desired to make one wise, she took of its fruit and ate and she also gave some to her husband and he ate. The eyes of both were opened and they knew they were naked and they sewed fig leaves together and made themselves aprons. And they heard the sound of the Lord God walking in the garden in the cool of the day and the man and his wife hid themselves from the presence of the Lord God among the trees of the garden.

The Hebrew word commonly translated serpent, *nâchâsh,* does not mean serpent, nor even devil. As a matter of fact, the word *nâchâsh* in Hebrew means to practice divination, and by extension, to shine. We might say the tempter was "a shining one." Later on the devil masquerades as an angel of light. I think there is a valid reason why the account does not make it clear that the devil caused Adam to sin. Our problem is not basically one of "the devil made me do it." The devil cannot make you or me do anything. He can tempt, he can distort, he can dazzle, he can suggest, but he can't "make us do it." Responsibility for sin is not the devil's—it is ours.

The tempter begins his conversation with Eve by distorting God's word. He asks her if God said not to eat any fruit in the garden (which is not what God said). The woman answers that God said, "You shall not eat of the fruit of the tree which is in the midst of the garden, neither shall you touch it, lest you die." The last half of her reply is utter fabrication. We find here the birth of legalism. The woman is, if you will, the first fundamentalist, the first circumcizer, the first

Pharisee who claims, "Grace is not enough. Grace operates only if certain rules are kept. It's not enough to love and obey God, we must follow some rigid code of behavior." The woman is really saying, "You see, we can't even touch the tree" (which God didn't say). Therefore God is a hard God. He is so exacting we can't possibly obey Him. The tempter and the woman have this dialogue founded entirely in lies. The tempter suggests that God has lied and that the woman cannot trust Him. The woman seems to reply, "You may be right. I hadn't thought about that."

As the woman examines the tree, she begins to ruminate about the benefits of eating its fruit. She decides the tree is good for food, that it is beautiful, and furthermore, its fruit would make her wise. In other words, by eating this fruit she and Adam will have it all. Her basic premise is that God doesn't want them to have it all. He cannot be trusted. That is still our problem as it was Eve's. Apparently she says, "I'm glad you pointed that out, shining one," and she and her husband make a conscious decision to disobey God and to eat.

The Myth of the Angry God

The last picture we'll entitle "The Myth of the Angry God." It is pivotal in terms of revealing who God is and who we are now. In Genesis 3:9 we find the Lord calling to the man and asking, "Where are you?" Adam answers, "I heard the sound of thee in the garden, and I was afraid, because I was naked; and I hid myself." God asks, "Who told you that you were naked? Have you eaten of the tree of which I commanded you not to eat?" The man's reply begins, "The woman" [he does not even call her Eve] "whom *thou* gavest . . ." He seems to be suggesting that God is responsible because He gave him this woman. It is all God's fault. "The woman whom *thou* gavest to be with me, she gave me the fruit of the tree and I ate."

When the Lord asks the woman, "What is this that you have done?" the woman says, "The serpent beguiled me, and I ate." That's called buck-passing. The myth concerns the nature of God. Man's problem is not his sin. That's God's problem and He has gone to great lengths to deal with it. Our disobedience in Eden, our disobedience today and yesterday cost God the death of His son. God has paid an unbelievable price to make reconciliation possible.

We hear a good many sermons that indicate that God knows what we're doing and we'd better repent and change. Yes, we need to repent, but God has not removed Himself because He can't tolerate our sinful ways. The New Testament speaks of the unforgivable sin, and that unforgivable sin is to call evil good and good evil. When we believe that God doesn't want to give us good things, the desires of our hearts, we are committing the unforgivable sin. That basic mistrust is the heart of evil and specific sins grow out of that basic mind set. When Adam and Eve sin against God, He is right back at the same place in the garden where He has always been waiting to walk with them. They're not there. They are hiding. Man, then and now, has removed himself from God, not God from man.

What a relentless friend God is! When you've blown it, when you've turned left when God said turn right, He goes left with you and continues to ask, "Where are you?" When God appears, He doesn't come to clobber you. He says, "You've grieved Me." God is more brokenhearted than angry. Right after Adam and Eve have sinned and made fig leaves and hidden themselves, God comes searching for them. He asks who is culpable and they pass the buck. Even after they confess their sins, Adam and Eve are not cursed. The shining one, or the tempter, is cursed. The ground from which we draw our sustenance is cursed.

When we doubt that God is our friend, we play games with Him. We see how much we can get away with. We commit sins of omission and commission. "Sins of omission," a little girl said, "are the sins I intended to commit, but never had time to." But, sin goes beyond cheating, lying, stealing, and all the rest. At its core it is not believing in God's goodness. We hide, we run, we play out scenarios in which we are always the injured party. We say, "Well, under the circumstances, what could I do? I'm innocent." Or, "All I said was ———, and she got mad." When we can stop maintaining our rightness and say that we are dishonest or mean or have hurt someone deliberately or otherwise, then God through Jesus Christ becomes our advocate.

What then are we to do? First of all, believe that God loves you. Admit that you're not the person you want to be and that you're being less than honest with some of the people in your life—your spouse, friends, parents. Trust God with your *now.* Come home. You can go back to Eden. That's what redemption is all about. Each of us has a *now* that we're struggling with. You may be single and lonely and growing older. That's a big now. Can you trust God with those fears? You may be out of work. Can you trust God with your job situation, your lack of funds? You may be in a job that's boring or not sufficiently challenging. Can you trust God with your future? If you're married, can you dare to tell your spouse some of your innermost feelings? Can you trust God with your health problems? Can you say, "I'm going to quit running my own life and I am going to trust You with my now"?

Yes, Eden is where it all began and where it all went awry. It is also the place where God demonstrated His plan for all of us. He created us for relationship with Him and nothing we do can make Him cease to be our friend.

3. Worship, Sacrifice, and Sacrilege

Genesis 4:1–16

How often have you heard someone say, "After all I've done for him (her, them), is this my reward?" It's a common and human plea. Most of us have, at some time or another, felt put upon or unappreciated. We have said that Genesis is the story of your life and mine, that its message is universal. In chapter 4 we see something of the rejection and the tragedy that is the experience of all of us some of the time, and some of us all of the time.

We have said that the Bible is written in right-brain language, that it is not primarily conceptual or theological, but rather somewhat like a picture book. As we look at the pictures in Genesis 4:1–16 and examine them with the intuitive, creative side of the brain, God can give us some profound insights into the human riddle.

Cain and Abel, the first two of Adam and Eve's many children, are worshiping. Worship throughout the Old Testament required sacrifice and that principle is still applicable today. If you worship your body, you must sacrifice time and energy in jogging, weight lifting, aerobic dancing. If you worship your car, you invest time and money and effort changing the oil, waxing, and otherwise maintaining it. If you worship your family you serve those loved ones with time and talent and money. These two young men understood

32

that to worship they must offer a sacrifice. Cain, the farmer, brought grain and his herdsman brother brought an animal, and the offering of grain was rejected.

Note again the personal nature of God. You can worship a machine, care for it, and keep it in good working order, but there is no way it can reject you. Only a personal God can react with joy or disapproval. In this chapter of Genesis, our Father Creator indicates that one offering won't do, while the other is pleasing.

It's hard to understand certain parts of this story. For instance, we are not told how they knew which offering was acceptable. We read in 1 Kings 19 about Elijah's confrontation with the priests of Baal. Both parties built altars and laid offerings on those altars. Elijah's offering for Jehovah was consumed by fire that came down from heaven, while the priests of Baal called on their gods in vain. It's possible that in those days if your offering pleased God a mysterious fire consumed it. That's one explanation. But we really don't know how God indicated His approval or disapproval in the case of Cain and Abel.

Motives for Murder

This is also history's first recorded murder, and it's an illogical one. Cain is angry with God for rejecting his offering, but he kills Abel. Abel didn't offend him. Abel simply made a pleasing sacrifice. I'm always puzzled by those stories in our newspapers about a murder in connection with a love triangle. Invariably, the irate mate comes on the scene and shoots the third person in the triangle. It would seem more appropriate to kill your mate. That's the person guilty of betrayal. But life is not logical and neither was the first murder. Cain is consumed by jealousy. He is outraged because he thinks God likes Abel best.

We find in this story an age-old theme where two siblings want to please their parent, in this case their eternal parent, and one is rejected. You may remember the Smothers Brothers used a routine playing on this theme. Tom would complain, "Mom always liked you best. How come when we both got pets, you got a dog and I got a chicken?" We laugh because the scenario strikes a familiar chord. In many families with more than one child, one may feel more special than the others.

In a fit of rage and jealousy, Cain strikes down his brother. But the surprising part is that even murder cannot separate God from His children. The murderer is found at the scene of his crime, blood dripping from his hands, and yet God is still his friend. Even murder can be forgiven and a relationship with God can be reestablished. We spoke earlier of the myth of the angry God. Our sins break God's heart. His wrath is real, but God's love is greater, and He is with us even in our worst moments. We can't hide from Him. That's who God is.

God's first words to Cain are not words of judgment but words of grace. He doesn't say, "Out of my sight, you murderer!" He simply asks, "Where is Abel, your brother?" Cain condemns himself with his arrogant and elusive answer. "Am I my brother's keeper?" The Hebrew word Cain uses for keeper is used primarily for animals rather than people. Shepherds were "keepers" of goats and sheep and all sorts of livestock. Cain is actually saying, "How should I know? Am I that shepherd's shepherd?" He is being a smart aleck with God and maintaining his innocence.

Responsible Guilt

At the heart of sin is our pretense of innocence. In God's Kingdom we are all responsibly guilty. Here are some poignant words about the human condition from John Steinbeck, one of my favorite writers. "The last clear statement of gallantry in my experience I heard in a state prison, a place for two-time losers, all lifers. In the yard an old hopeless convict spoke as follows: 'The kids come up here and they bawl how they wasn't guilty, or how they was framed, or how it was their mother's fault or their father was a drunk.' Us old boys tell them, 'Kid, for God's sake, do your own time and let us do ours.' " These wise oldtimers understand how futile it is to blame somebody else for your predicament or insist on your innocence. Owning up to your guilt is the first step in the long voyage home.

There is another lesson for us in this dialogue between God and Cain. To be responsible before God means being responsible for our brother. It is not enough to say we love God. He asks us, as He did Cain, "Where is your brother?" Where is your brother in your city or town? Where is your brother in Cambodia or Central America? We avoid our responsibility and say, "Am I that shepherd's shepherd?" But God holds us accountable for the brothers and sisters around us in our neighborhood or in the world. We have said that the two great themes interwoven all through Genesis are law and grace. Cain is dealt with under the law. The first murderer is banished from the place and from the face of the Lord. And yet God's love goes with him.

I spent my study leave in Hawaii a year or two ago and I read an interesting item in the Honolulu papers one morning. A Samoan man had been murdered and his family was holding the "ceremony of forgiveness" which the article described as "traditional." I'd love to find out more about that ceremony. In a traditional ceremony, the murdered man's family forgives his murderer. A judge, nevertheless, had sentenced that man to one and a half years in prison with an additional five or ten years on parole. Even though we are forgiven by God or by those we've offended, there are inescapable consequences under the law.

The Mark of God

Cain is banished and he is distraught. He says, "My punishment is greater than I can bear. Behold, thou hast driven me this day away from the ground; and from thy face I shall

be hidden; and I shall be a fugitive and a wanderer on the
earth, and whoever finds me will slay me." Cain is certain
he will be killed in his exile and, even worse, he will be
hidden from God's presence, which is what hell is all about.
Hearing Cain's plea, God acts in mercy. "The Lord said to
him, 'Not so! If anyone slays Cain, vengeance shall be taken
on him sevenfold.' And the Lord put a mark on Cain, lest
any who came upon him should kill him." Cain is banished,
but God sends him off with words of grace. Genesis tells
us he went off to dwell in the Land of Nod, where he was
to become the patriarch of a whole family of shepherds, musi-
cians, and craftsmen.

You and I have God's mark on us just as visibly if we
are believers. Even when we have committed the worst possible sins, the mark of Jesus Christ and His atonement is on
us. God's grace is operating, even when we break the law.
I heard about two young brothers in a sheepherding village
who were caught stealing sheep. The punishment given at
that time was a brand on the forehead with the letters "ST"
for sheep thief. One man fled the village and spent his remaining years wandering from place to place. When the meaning
of his brand was discovered, he was in immediate disgrace
and forced to move on. He lived his whole life as an outcast.
His brother, on the other hand, remained in his home town
and made restitution for the stolen sheep. In the ensuing
years he tried to be a responsible, caring friend and neighbor.
He lived to be a very old man, loved by all. The story is
told that one day a stranger came to town and inquired about
the "ST" on this old man's forehead. "I'm not sure what it
means," he was told. "It all happened so long ago. But I
think that those letters stand for 'saint.'"

An Acceptable Offering

What does the story of Cain and Abel mean? Both of these
men are believers. They're not worshiping material goods,

family, success, careers, or money. They are authentically worshiping God. We might conclude that the nature of the sacrifice is the issue. Some would say that the Bible is clear that there is no remission of sin apart from the shedding of blood. While Abel laid a sheep on the altar, we might speculate that Cain brought twenty-seven bushels of zucchini. We know he offered something he raised from the land. Personally, I do not think the nature of the object he offered is the issue because in latter days the Israelites were not all ranchers or shepherds. Farmers could trade their produce for a turtledove, a sheep, or a goat. Furthermore, in Psalms 51:17 we read, "The sacrifice acceptable to God is a broken spirit."

Perhaps Cain's offering was too small, but I don't think that was the problem. The New Testament story of the widow's mite indicates that the amount of the offering is not important. We have another example of a pleasing offering in the book of Acts. Barnabas sold a piece of land and brought all the proceeds to the disciples to be used for God's work.

Whether our offering is very little or very much, the key factor is our attitude. God looks on the heart of the giver. Perhaps Cain, through pride, gave a more expensive offering than Abel, hoping to prove he was a more devout man than Abel. We read in the New Testament about a woman who poured expensive ointment over Jesus' feet, an act considered by the disciples a needless extravagance. Judas objected on the grounds that it was wasteful and the money should go to the poor. And yet Jesus seemed to be pleased by her offering.

On the other hand, perhaps Cain was trying to get by with giving as little as possible. In the church I serve, each prospective new member is interviewed by one of our thirty-six elders. Recently one elder was asked, "What does it cost to belong to this church?" "Nothing," was the reply, which is true only in the sense that there are no set dues. Nevertheless, we Christians are to be stewards of all that we have and are. Some people want to know how little they can give and still be acceptable. Others ask, "What's my share?" That's just as inappropriate. God looks beyond the amount or nature of our gift and perceives why we are giving. Possibly, Cain gave his offering to God conditionally, hoping to manipulate Him. Cain might have been attempting to win God's favor and blessing by means of his offering.

I've met people like that. They have served God faithfully for years as teachers, church leaders, and even tithers until some tragedy strikes, such as the illness or death of a family member. They leave the church and the faith because they feel God has let them down. They were giving and serving all those years to put God in their debt. They are incensed when God doesn't keep His part of the bargain. Unfortunately, life is unpredictable for all of us, Christians and non-Christians. We don't get what we deserve. On an occasion when Jack Benny, one of my favorite twentieth-century comedians, was given an award he said in accepting it, "I really don't deserve this award. But then, I have arthritis, and I don't deserve that either." When you go through life thinking you deserve God's favor because of your performance, you've missed the Christian message.

The Spirit of Sacrifice

Perhaps we may find a clue to the underlying dynamic of the story in the names given these brothers. Cain (*Qayin* in Hebrew) may come from *qanah,* and could mean "begotten," or, by extension, "longed for," "loved." Based on a different root, it may also mean "ironworker" or "spear." It's a strong name, a special name. Abel comes from the Hebrew *hebel,* meaning a "slight breath" or "frail," figuratively, "empty" or "in vain." A family may have a strong child and a frail child, or, perhaps, a gifted child and an ordinary child, and then, however careful they are, parents seem to say to one child, "Wow, you are really something!" while the other feels like an also-ran. In Cain and Abel's case, perhaps Cain is convinced of his superiority and importance, while his brother feels inadequate. In that spirit of unworthiness and humility, Abel offers his gift of love to God.

Almost all of us have had the experience of being a guest at a party. Every party represents a sacrificial offering on the part of the host and hostess. They clean the house, polish the silver, get out the best china, and spend time preparing food. Some hosts and hostesses have a need to let you know how hard they have worked to do all this, and that's not much fun for the guests. On the other hand, there are those parties that required just as much effort, and yet the host and hostess seem to have done it all with ease and even joy. In the second case, the hosts communicate verbally and nonverbally, "Thanks for coming. What a privilege to have you here. You made the party." Even the less sensitive among us can detect when that sort of social sacrificial offering is made in a spirit of joy and thanksgiving. We shouldn't be surprised that God can perceive the spirit behind our giving. He is aware of our motives.

We've all heard the motto "Give 'Til It Hurts." But if it hurts us to give, we are doing it in the wrong spirit, in an attempt to put someone, even God, in our debt. I suggest we give until it feels good, give until we can say, "I am so privileged to be able to do this." That kind of offering is pleasing to God.

The gift of life comes from God and it cannot be hoarded. Life is fragile and its end unpredictable. But that should not frighten or intimidate us in terms of giving sacrificially. If we were as rich as Bunky Hunt and had the endless life of a vampire, our giving would be meaningless. In this world, most of us don't have enough time or an overabundance of possessions. Out of those scarce commodities, we give to God and to others, and that's what sacrifice is all about. Someone has captured the world's predicament with this analogy: "Suppose the world were reduced to a global village of one hundred people. Eighty of them would be unable to read,

only one of those people would have a college education,
fifty would be suffering from malnutrition, and eighty would
be found living in houses unfit for human habitation. In this
same village of one hundred, six would be Americans who
have one half of the entire income of the village, leaving
the remaining ninety-four to exist on the other fifty percent."
God is still asking us, as He did Cain, "Where is your brother
(and sister)?" A good many of us say, "How do I know?
I'm just busy making a living." But to come before God
responsibly, we must confess our guilt and our responsibility.
We could do more. We'd like to do more. God help us to
do more.

Eternal Treasures

In thinking about all this, a strange thought occurred to me.
Many years ago when my wife Hazel and I were struggling
financially, we decided to give her mother an expensive gift.
We were leading a tour to the Holy Land, and in Jerusalem
we bought her a beautiful eighteen-carat gold cross which
she wore for all her remaining years. A year or so later, I
saw in a magazine a picture of some children doing Swedish
folk-dancing in the streets of Lindsborg, Kansas. I knew my
mother would love that picture. I have never before or since
commissioned any original art, but I wrote to the artist and
asked her to reproduce that picture for my mother for her
birthday. My mother was simply delighted with it.

Both of those dear women are now dead. One morning
as we were sitting having coffee in our kitchen, I noticed
Hazel wearing the gold cross that we had given her mother.
On the wall of the family room portion of the kitchen is
the picture we couldn't afford. Both of those sacrificial gifts
are now our possessions. I thought to myself that this might
be a preview of eternity. Your heavenly home may be furnished with all the things you have given away in this life.
Those things are somehow eternal, while the things we keep

for ourselves are transitory. The Bible speaks of storing up for yourselves treasures in heaven, and perhaps that's how it works. In Westminster Abbey, the 1680 tomb of Christopher Chapman reads: "What I gave I have. What I spent I had. What I left I lost by not giving it."

The Cain and Abel story is full of pathos. How puzzling that this portion of Genesis gives us an account of the first formal act of worship followed by the world's first violent crime. We can speculate endlessly on why Abel's gift was acceptable and Cain's was not. The fact remains that in the very act of worshiping, Cain's jealousy overcame him and he slew his brother. God had created His children capable of love and hatred, sacrifice and brutality. The astonishing thing is that even in the midst of it all, we perceive the loving, forgiving nature of our Creator and friend.

4. An Ark for All Seasons

Genesis 6

What a treasure the story of old Noah and his ark has been to whole generations of children and adults. We just never seem to exhaust its depths and all its colorful implications. Think of the toymakers who have been kept from bankruptcy by all of those arks and animals of plastic and wood which children over the centuries have enjoyed. Where would comedian Bill Cosby be without Noah? His marvelous depiction of the dialogue between God and Noah and Noah and his neighbors is a pretty fair up-to-date version of the way it was.

Certainly, there is no shortage of cartoons and jokes about Noah and the flood. Several years ago a man gave me this piece which he claims was read at a very prestigious, high-level business meeting.

The Lord said to Noah, "Where is the ark I commanded you to build?" And Noah said, "Verily, I had three carpenters off sick, and the gopherwood supplier hath let me down, even though gopherwood hath been on order for nigh on twelve months." And God said to Noah, "I want the ark finished before seven days and seven nights," and Noah said, "It will be so," and it was not so. The Lord said to Noah, "What seems to be the trouble this time?" And Noah said, "My subcontractor hath gone bankrupt, the pitch for the outside hath not arrived, the

glazer departeth on holiday, yea even though I offered him double time. Lord, I am undone." The Lord grew angry and said,
"What about the animals? Two of every sort I ordered. Where
are the giraffes?" And Noah said, "They have been delivered
to the wrong address but should arrive on Friday." The Lord
said to Noah, "How about the unicorns?" Noah wrung his hands
and wept, "Oh, Lord, they are a discontinued line. Thou canst
not get unicorns for love or money. Thou knowest how it is."
And the Lord said, "Noah, my son, I know. Why else dost
thou think I caused the flood?"

The Noah's Ark story is perhaps the most widely known
Old Testament story to believers and unbelievers, alike. But
its very familiarity can prevent us from grasping its signifi-
cance, for nowhere do we see God's mind revealed more
clearly than in this particular story. In it we find again the
major threads or themes mentioned earlier, of God's wrath
and God's grace, of man's belief and his unbelief, and of
the unbreakable friendship God offers.

God's Breaking Point

The primal truth in this particular story is obvious: evil
abounds and God is displeased and broken-hearted because
of it. I serve on a college board, and at a recent meeting
the dean of housing was discussing the problem of handling
infractions of the rules. "We have discovered," he said, "that
there is a clumping syndrome for sin." He went on to explain,
"We find that students seldom have only one infraction. They
figure as long as they have broken one rule they might as
well break others." In the story of Noah, God sees this clumping syndrome at loose in the whole inhabited world. Sin
abounds and continues. And is it too anthropomorphic to
believe that God actually came to the place where He could
no longer endure this world He had created? Haven't you
felt like that sometimes when you've taken a good, hard look
at the world and its evils?

During World War II, my infantry outfit liberated the Dachau concentration camp. I've been back there twice since with pilgrims and have seen the silver monument which the Germans have erected to remind them of the evil that lurks in the hearts of all people. There is also a Holocaust Museum in Jerusalem which is a sober memorial to the horrors of the death camps. Places like that are piercing reminders of man's inhumanity to his brothers and sisters. We can understand that at some point in history God might have said, "I can't take it any more. I shall destroy this creation which has gone so far awry."

God is a God of law, and when we break those laws, destruction comes and wars erupt, primarily because we don't know enough about love or forgiveness. We transgress sexual and moral laws and diseases result, some of which have no known cures. We flout God's laws and bring destruction upon ourselves. But, wherever there is belief, there is grace. There was for Noah. In Genesis 6:8 we read, "Noah found favor. . . ." In this terrible world where sin is clumping at a furious pace, God looks out and sees one faithful and righteous man, the kind of man He had in mind when He made the human race. He decides to save him. Grace overcomes the law. Now, lest you bring some Victorian preconception to what all this means, let me say that I do not believe God saved Noah for his moral purity or his sinlessness. Later on (after the flood) we find Noah gets dead drunk and sleeps naked in a fairly public place to the embarrassment of his sons. Nevertheless, in Noah God found one faithful man who understood Him, who believed in Him, and who was trying to live his life accordingly as God's friend.

Dimensions for Salvation

For this man, then, God designed salvation, and that's noteworthy. *We* don't design salvation. We are not saved by our worship or offerings or rituals or even our theological beliefs.

God is the author of salvation. There was no salvation for Noah apart from an ark of very exact and precise dimensions. Noah's salvation was to be 450 feet long and 75 feet wide and 45 feet deep. It was to be constructed of gopherwood. Nobody quite knows what gopherwood is, but the word *gopher* comes from the Hebrew word for *covering* and *pitch* comes from that same root. Evidently, it's a material that both covers and seals. Noah obeyed God and began construction of the huge ark on dry land.

Just imagine somebody today starting to build an ark of those same enormous dimensions in some land-locked place, miles from any water. A project of that scope would take years. All the while, the neighbors would be saying what Bill Cosby has them saying on his famous record. "Will you get that thing out of your driveway? It's blocking my view. What's all this constant sawing and hammering?" People must have been hooting and jeering because Noah was building this ridiculous structure in this unlikely place where it could not possibly be used. Noah listened to God instead, who said, "Build it. Build it here and build it my way." He followed God in spite of what his neighbors thought. That's what righteousness is all about, Noah's story is telling us. We live God's way in spite of what our families or neighbors say. Sometimes, like Noah, we become objects of ridicule.

In these present times, we Christians are a minority in the land. God has given us laws about our sex life. We're not to be promiscuous. We are to be chaste and pure and faithful within the marriage relationship. That makes us a minority. The world says, "Come on, get with it." Because of our faith, we are to be honest in all our dealings. But that's not how the world lives. We are urged instead, "Take care of Number One. Do whatever you can get away with." Often we find ourselves objects of ridicule, but we live this way because we believe in an invisible God who has told us to, and we do it in simple faith.

Acting in Faith

Noah built his enormous ark on dry land in spite of the derision of his neighbors, and eventually he was vindicated. The flood did come, a flood of overwhelming vastness. In addition to the Bible, most of the literature of early peoples tells of a great flood that covered all the known world. You might well ask, "Where did all that water come from?" The Bible does give us some clues. Genesis 7:11 says: ". . . All the fountains of the great deep burst forth and the windows of the heavens were opened." "Fountains of the great deep bursting forth" would suggest volcanos and earthquakes that would have raised the sea level hundreds or even thousands of feet. Another theory is that a great cloud cover over the earth opened up and produced endless rain. (The possibility has even been considered that a meteorite came near the earth and tipped it on its axis, causing the waters of the earth to cover vast areas of its surface. Thousands of perfectly preserved dinosaurs and other animals have been found frozen in the northern recesses of our world. There is conjecture that these originally inhabited tropical regions when a tilt of the earth resulted in a great ice age.)

But here's the part I like best—it is the heart of what faith is all about. Seven days before the first drop of rain, God tells Noah and his family to get in the ark with the animals. God Himself seals the door; Noah does not close it. (It's a powerful analogy. I like to think we present-day Christians have been sealed into the Ark of the Covenant. In baptism, God has put His seal on us.) Imagine the scene. For seven days the sun is shining and all of the neighbors are outside laughing it up, barbecuing, playing badminton, while the braying of donkeys, the honking of geese, the bellowing of elephants emanate from inside this ark. We can imagine their conversation. "Can you believe that crazy Noah? The sun is shining and there he is, locked in his boat with all that livestock." Noah and his family are forced to listen to all these derogatory comments when suddenly the rain starts and the scene changes. For the crowd outside the ark, the water is soon up to their ankles, then up to their knees, and eventually over their heads. Too late for repentance.

Noah and his family stayed in the ark through the rain and the floods for 150 days until finally they hit dry land. The ark had been their salvation, and apart from it, they couldn't have made it. But when the flood was over they had to leave. To stay in the ark would have meant death. Again we have a parallel for Christian salvation. The new ark is Jesus Christ. Apart from Him there is no salvation from the world's sin and rejection. We come to Him. But having come to Him, He sends us out into a new life. We cannot hunker down in a safe place.

What is the first thing Noah does after the flood? He builds an altar and offers an animal in sacrifice to God. As it's burning on the altar, we are told, the aroma is pleasing to God, for He delights in the sacrifices of His people. This is yet another truth in this fascinating story. Even now as you give your tithes and pledges week by week and as the scent of that gift goes up, God says, "That pleases me." That's the invisible dimension of faith—to believe that you have the power to please God.

By means of the rainbow, God makes a covenant with Noah and all of the human race. The rainbow is a sign of God's promise that the flood will never be repeated. Noah and his family went forth from the ark to a world full of bloated corpses and the stench of rotting vegetation. The waters were receding, leaving only devastation behind. Those who survived in the ark were sent back into that world to regenerate and reproduce. The same law and grace we see at work in the story of Noah are still at work today. Our world is full of sin and the stench of bloated corpses, but where there is belief and righteousness, grace is operating.

Still another truth in this chapter is the definition of

righteousness it gives us. We learn that righteousness is believing God and doing what He tells us to do, in spite of what our neighbors say or in spite of how the world lives. Righteousness is trust and *obedience*, not sinlessness. Sinlessness is not within our capacity. David was an adulterer, liar, murderer, and thief. But God called him "a man after my own heart." David confessed his sin publicly and tried to make restitution; he believed in God and tried to serve Him. Abraham, who started a journey to an unknown destination in obedience to God, is called the father of the faithful. Paul was obedient to the heavenly vision. Obedience is what righteousness is, and sometimes it seems silly, like building an ark in the middle of a desert.

The New Ark

Righteousness never makes sense to the unbeliever. God is still calling us to the building of the ark. The new ark is Jesus Christ and His church and we are called to build His body. There is no way Noah could have been saved apart from the ark. There's no salvation for us apart from the new ark. Where is it? It's the brothers and sisters around us in the household of God. We have the temerity to believe that this is the body of Christ in the world, and if we can see that, we have the gift of faith. Yes, there are problems. Certainly the ark had its problems. Someone has said, "If it wasn't for the storm outside you couldn't stand the smell inside." Just think about 150 days with a herd of assorted animals—elephants, monkeys, etc. But the alternative was death. With all of our problems, the church is the family of faith and our salvation comes as we build the ark, a congregation of people in whom Christ lives.

We can choose not to understand. We can be like the office manager opening the employees' suggestion box. After reading a few suggestions, he looks up and says, "I wish they could be more specific. What kind of a kite and what lake?" We can choose not to know what God has made clear in terms of salvation, but He is still sending the message as He did to Noah. The New Testament message is that there is no other name given under heaven whereby we can be saved but Jesus Christ. We are to come unto Him, into the new covenant, into the ark, an ark for all seasons.

Hearing the Message

Having heard that message, there are particular messages of how we are to live our lives. God is trying to talk to us about our professions, our jobs, our friendships, our family, our finances, every part of our lives. That's why we keep a prayer time with our Bibles open, our notebooks ready. We can hear those messages at any time, even driving down the freeway. Obedience to those messages is what righteousness is all about. And we trust God even when we don't entirely understand. It's too late to build an ark after the rain hits.

In George Bernard Shaw's *St. Joan,* his heroine speaks of hearing God's messages. I have a hard time believing that old George Bernard Shaw, that brilliant skeptic, wrote such powerful lines. In his play, Joan of Arc is talking to King Charles. She is a constant annoyance to him and he doesn't appreciate this crazy lady in armor who insists on leading armies. He says, "Oh, your voices, your voices, always your voices. Why don't the voices come to me? I am king, not you." Joan replies, "They do come to you, but you do not hear them. You have not sat in the field in the evening listening for them. When the Angelus rings you cross yourself and have done with it. But, if you prayed from your heart and listened to the trilling of the bells in the air after they stop ringing, you would hear the voices as well as I do." Joan heard voices and believed that God was speaking to her.

The industrialist Andrew Carnegie was once interviewed about the reason for his success. He said, "I owe it all to my flashes.". When asked to explain that, he said, "All of my life I woke up early in the morning and always there came into my mind with the waking a flash telling me what to do that day. And if I followed those morning flashes I always succeeded." "You mean," said the interviewer, "you've been having heavenly visions?" "You call it what you will," Carnegie replied, "but it was the following of those silent admonitions and directions which brought me to the success you say I've achieved."

We know the message for salvation—Jesus Christ Himself. We are to build His body, the new ark, and be a part of God's household. The ark saves us but we can't live forever in the ark. You and I must go out into that world full of rotting corpses and bring regeneration, creativity, and newness of life. As we said, we can't stay in the ark, the new ark, permanently, but we are to come back regularly. The church is an ark for all seasons. We are saved by God's grace. The design of His salvation is the body and blood of His Son. From this ark, we are to go out, as Noah did, to regenerate and reproduce.

5. Breaking the Sound Barrier

Genesis 11

I'm sure that I'm not alone in feeling that language has been the cause of more frustrations and embarrassments in my life than almost anything else. Language, this marvelous vehicle for communication, can be so frustrating.

I moved to south Florida about ten years ago after a lifetime of being a Yankee. One afternoon I was having difficulty finding a certain place of business in the town of Fort Myers, and I stopped to ask for help from a native south Floridian. She gave me directions and I said, "Will you repeat that, please?" She said it all again, and once more I had to ask her to repeat it. Finally, I just said, "Thanks," and moved on, hoping I was going in the direction she was trying to suggest. I didn't want to embarrass her. Two citizens of the same country with a common language were unable to communicate. Maybe you've been in a foreign country and found yourself unable to communicate some urgent need. Most of us tend to speak louder. We shout out, "Where is the bathroom?" but still nobody responds.

Language is a mystery. Language unites and divides. Language is revealing. A friend of mine has done research on how people of different nationalities answer the telephone. His conclusions are interesting. We Americans say, "Hello." I won't attempt to give a rationale for that. Germans, how-

ever, answer the phone by giving their full name. "Frieda
Baumgartner Horstwessel." The French reverse that process
and demand to know, "Who's on the line?" Italians greet
callers with "Ready." Englishmen ask, "Are you there?" And
Russians simply declare, "I'm listening." Make of that valuable research what you will.

In the past, there have been many attempts to solve our
language problems. Years ago someone invented a language
called "Esperanto." The idea was to eliminate communication
problems by creating a common language that all the world's
people would learn. The United Nations had another solution. The delegates, using earphones, could hear the speaker
in his or her native language. It was a great device, but it
didn't solve our communication problems at the United Nations.

Monuments, Then and Now

In the Old Testament, a common language is the cause of
man's ultimate folly, the building of the Tower of Babel.
Genesis 11 gives us the story. An early race of people with
one language were living at peace on the plain in Shinar
(Babylonia) and they undertook to build themselves a city
of brick, dominated by a tower reaching to the heavens. Their
reasons for doing so were two-fold: they wanted to be a
more united, cohesive group and they desired to "make a
name for ourselves" (v. 4). They were working for fame
and self-sufficiency. The city and the tower were such an
affront to the Lord that He said, "Come, let us go down
and there confuse their language, that they may not understand one another's speech." The result is that they were
suddenly scattered over the face of the earth and were no
longer united by a common language. The worship of self
ended in alienation and separation.

This tower is thought to have been a seven-layered ziggurat
built on a mound. It was erected to show man's potential,

but it became a monument to his own achievements, inventiveness, and self-reliance. Theologian Derek Kidner says of the Tower of Babel: "Primeval history reaches its fruitless climax as man, conscious of new abilities, prepares to glorify and fortify himself by collective effort."

That was just the first of man's efforts down through the ages to erect monuments to himself. The Egyptians attempted to convince the world that they had conquered death itself in their mighty pyramids. The glorious architecture and culture of Greece was the Tower of Babel of its time. Next came the splendor and might of Rome. More recently, the British were fond of reminding themselves that "the sun never sets on the British Empire." It did! Hitler bragged that the Third Reich would last for a thousand years. It lasted only a few years, years of horror and tragedy for the whole world.

Those of us in the Western world, particularly in America, are erecting our own Towers of Babel. We have our technology and our nuclear weapons and we surround ourselves with our own creations and retreat behind them, secure in our own might. There's a lesson for us in the story of the famous Maginot Line, where the French invested billions of dollars in order to prove to the world that no enemy could possibly penetrate their borders. In a matter of days, the Nazi Panzers did just that.

The lesson of the Tower of Babel is that when man worships himself and his achievements, communication is hopeless, even with a common language. The ability to hear each other still eludes us as husbands and wives, as parents and children, or as nations. With one language or many we still don't communicate.

Language Problems

Language is reduced to jargon in the various disciplines. Lawyers speak legalese; teachers have teacherese. Doctors use medicalese and preachers rely on theologicalese—usually delivered in funereal or stentorian tones. Here an anonymous author has penned some notes from a psychiatric social worker:

> I never get mad; I get hostile.
> I never feel sad; I'm depressed.
> If I sew and knit and enjoy it a bit,
> I'm not handy; I'm really upset.
> I never regret; I feel guilty.
> And if I should vacuum the hall,
> wash the woodwork and such and not mind it too much,
> am I tidy?
> Compulsive is all.
> If I can't choose a hat, I have conflicts.
> With ambivalent feelings toward it,
> I never get nervous or hurried; anxiety, that's what I get.
> If I get happy, I must be euphoric,
> If I go to the Stork Club and Ritz
> and have a good time making puns or rhyme,
> I'm a manic, or maybe a schiz.
> If I tell you you're right, I'm submissive,
> repressing aggressiveness too.
> And when I disagree I'm defensive, you see,
> and projecting my symptoms on you.
> I love you, but that's just transference
> with Oedipus rearing its head.
> My breathing asthmatic is psychosomatic,
> a fear of exclaiming "drop dead!"
> I'm not lonely; I'm simply dependent.
> My dog has no fleas, just a tic.
> So, if I'm a cad, never mind, just be glad
> I'm not a stinker; I'm sick.

That kind of language is a way of using new words to say all the same old things.

But sometimes the words are perfectly clear, and you still don't get the message. A kindergarten teacher friend of mine told me about an experience like that. She lives in a place where snowsuits are often required. One day she was, with much difficulty, helping a little boy into his snowsuit. It was one of those infernal ones with snaps, ties, and buttons. The only way she could manage was to have him lie flat on the floor while she pushed and pulled and tugged and snapped. When she finally got him in, he looked up at her and said, "This isn't my snowsuit." With the grace and patience divinely given to kindergarten teachers, she helped him out of the snowsuit. He continued his story. "This is my sister's snowsuit. My mother said I could wear it today."

Babel has become the symbol of the self-worship which separates and alienates us from each other. If there is any lesson in the story of Babel, it is that man's own efforts, apart from God, are futile. Our smarts and our technology will not save our nation or any nation. The only thing that will save us, personally and nationally, is a revival where God's Spirit enters individuals and churches and nations.

The Gift of Hearing

That's what happened at Pentecost. We read in the second chapter of Acts that, at the time, citizens from every known nation in the world were in Jerusalem. Every language was being used in that city when God poured out His Spirit. Yet for those who experienced that event, language was not a barrier. Each person heard in his or her own tongue. God broke the sound barrier and from then on direct communication with our Creator-friend was possible.

The Pentecost story indicates that communication depends on hearing, not on language. When your heart is centered in God, you are able to hear with new understanding. The miracle of Pentecost is that those whose hearts were centered in God were now able to communicate to their neighbors and friends and even to strangers.

A couple in our congregation went to Cambodia several

years ago. Jim served as a doctor and his wife as a nursing
assistant in a refugee camp. At the end of their long and
exhausting days, Jim and Ann took time to sit outside on
what was called "the hugging bench." Children and even
some oldsters came, just to sit and experience love, the ultimate communication. Words were unnecessary. A team of
adults went out from our church to meet Christians from
behind the Iron Curtain one summer. They speak very little
German, and the Germans couldn't speak much English. But
they were able to make themselves understood. Their witness
to Christ was at the center of their communication and they
overcame language barriers.

Our Pastor of Missions and one of our elders returned
recently from a visit with perhaps as primitive a people as
exist in the world today, the Masai of East Africa. These
two somewhat urbane, sophisticated Seattleites spent many
days with these proud warriors, with their elongated ears,
strange tribal dress, beads, and spears. Culturally, they were
millions of miles apart, but because of Jesus Christ they had
common concerns and communication took place. They
talked about the needs of their children, and culture and
language were transcended.

You may have gone at some time to a Marriage Encounter
or Engaged Encounter weekend. It's a wonderful experience
for couples who are having difficulty communicating. The
weekend centers in worshiping God, with the result that
couples begin to open their hearts to each other. As God's
Spirit permeates everyone in this environment, language is
often unnecessary. Couples who have been strangers to each
other fall in love again. They discover that the basic problem was never communication but, rather, the worship of
self—two people each trying to use the other for his or her
own ends.

When God is the center of a shared experience, we become
one, and God gives Himself to us. Saint Exupery wrote in
Wind, Sand and Stars, "Love does not consist of gazing at

each other, but of looking outward in the same direction."
Two people staring only at each other, or two nations con-
fronting each other only from positions of invulnerability and
self-interest can't communicate. We break the sound barrier
only when we look outward to our Creator-friend who is
the source of our life and redemption.

6. Hearing God's Call

Genesis 12

A while back a man made an appointment with me to talk about his son. He said, "I'm not a member of your church. As a matter of fact, I'm an atheist, but I need your help. My son, who is an honor student at the university and a member of this church, tells me that he has a call from the Lord. What exactly is that?"

For the next two hours we talked about what constitutes a call from the Lord and what it is not. It is not, for example, a commitment to disseminate and propagate Christian theology and morality and biblical teachings. The desire to do all that cannot be considered a call. A call can come only from a person. Faith is our response to a personal call. That's the difference between faith and belief. Belief alone can't be equated with a call. Faith is not belief in spite of evidence but life lived in scorn of consequences. I told this puzzled father, "Your son has heard God's particular and personal call to follow Him and he must sort that out and find the specific area in which he is to do that."

Christians have so much to be thankful for in terms of the Judeo-Christian heritage. But I feel especially grateful for all those on whose shoulders we stand, those who have heard God's call. They have given us a priceless inheritance. Think about them. They are the patriarchs, prophets, apostles,

martyrs, saints like Francis or Teresa, reformers like Luther
and Calvin and Knox, and all the rest. As a Presbyterian, I
feel grateful for those old Scottish covenanters who risked
their very lives to worship God.

America was settled by the Pilgrims who left Great Britain
in response to a call from God. They came to this new land
in order to be free to hear and follow God's call. We salute
them for their faith and bravery. But among all those heroes
of the faith, let's bear in mind that Abraham was the first
person to hear God's call. In response to that call to follow
God, he became an immigrant, a wanderer in a strange land,
and his story in Genesis points up some particular dimensions
of the call of God.

A Personal Call

First of all, it is a person-to-person call. Abraham, who was
limited as we are, heard a message from an invisible God.
How incredible that he would respond as he did. He had
no Bible, no church, no support from the fellowship of believers, no spiritual history, and no role model. He had none
of the resources that we have now to help us understand
and follow God's call. From somewhere in infinity God
crashes through to this first spiritual pioneer and tells him
to leave his home and start a journey—*and he does.*

The call from God is always a right-brain call and, as we
said earlier, the Bible is essentially a right-brain book. When
we are relating person to person, not concept to concept,
we're using the same instinctive, intuitive, non-rational side
of the brain that we use when we fall in love and give
ourselves to another person. An encounter with God is a
right-brain encounter in which He makes Himself known
to us and we respond as did Abraham. The call of God has
nothing to do with logic, reason, equations, statistics, or
charts. It is a call from a person—and that person is God
Himself.

A Call to the Unknown

In examining this first call of God to Abraham, we see that it is a call from the safety and security of the familiar to the unknown, the unsafe, and the uncertain. That's the very essence of a genuine call from God. God tells Abraham to go from his country, his kindred, and his father's house, three separate entities.

First, he is to leave his country. Our country represents a culture and a culture shapes values. Values are reflected in friends and clubs, investments and bank accounts, careers and hobbies, movies, books, and TV shows. Next, Abraham is to leave his kindred. This archaic word simply means tribe or clan. In today's terms, it would be those who gather together for holidays and special celebrations. Simply, it's home and home has been described as the place you can go when you've failed and they've got to take you in. Your kindred is that tribe and clan to whom you belong by birth—your roots. God's call, in this case, requires leaving all that behind.

Third, Abraham is told to leave his father's house. In the Middle East, your father's house gives you your identity in a special way. Your inheritance, your birthright, your security, all of these things are yours automatically because you belong to your father's house. My wife has that kind of secure identity, and I've always envied it. She grew up in a small town of about 1,500 residents on the Hudson River. In that town everybody is known and everybody has a particular place. We go back there occasionally to visit family, and when I meet someone at the drugstore on Main Street, they invariably say, "I know you. You're the guy that married George Fischer's youngest daughter." That's my identity in that town, and will be forever. Being a part of your father's house in the ancient tribal times of Abraham meant all of that and much more. God's call to Abraham was away from country, kindred, and his father's house into the unknown; from predictability to risk and danger.

A Call to Trust

Responding to God's call means finding our security in God alone. Abraham had to believe that God would do what He promised, that He would, in fact, "bless those who bless you and curse those who curse you, and by you all the families of the earth shall bless themselves." On the strength of that, Abraham left his country, his kindred, and his father's house and launched out. His only certainty was in the belief that God was who He said He was and would do what He said He would do. It's the kind of blind trust that Noah demonstrated when he undertook the building of a great ship to float in the sea with no sign of an imminent flood. How do you suppose Abraham explained his action to his neighbors? Imagine the dialogue.

"I am buying a few camels and some donkeys and we're packing up."

"Where are you going?"

"Where God leads."

"God? Which god? We've got lots of gods right here in Ur. We have temples full of gods. What are you talking about?"

I'm sure there was no way Abraham could explain his actions. He acted in trust and his culture, his society, his friends and family must have thought he was deranged. Abraham did not know why or where he was going or how to get there. There was no road map. God seemed to say, "Start off and when you get to a crossroad, I'll guide you right or left." It sounded crazy, but, like all visionaries, he believed the incredible and he saw the invisible and he attempted the impossible, and, of course, we are the heirs of that act of faith.

Authentic visionaries are often people like Abraham who do not seem to need the usual security blankets. They bet on the vision and the God who gave that vision. I mentioned earlier that while I was in seminary at Princeton I used to

live near Dr. Albert Einstein. When he was invited to join
their Institute for Advanced Studies there, he was asked what
kind of salary he would require. "I don't know," was the
reply. "Talk to my wife." He never knew how much he
was paid. His wife took care of those details. He was caught
up in his vision and had no interest in or concern for the
mundane details of wages and pension plans.

Friends of mine in the Midwest live in a great manor house
built three generations ago by an illustrious ancestor, a mer-
chant prince. As a young man he had built the first stagecoach
route through his state. This great house was filled with treasures he had collected. Four generations later, his descendants
have become museum-keepers for that collection. It seems
to me we all have that sort of choice in life. We can be the
builder, the prophet, the visionary who gathers treasures,
or we can be the one who reveres and maintains trophies
somebody else has gathered. I would suggest there is more
to life than being a curator for somebody else's treasures,
and that is to get out and get our own. Let somebody else
worry about dusting and polishing them.

I've observed a number of organizations, particularly para-
church organizations, who have gone through this metamor-
phosis from pioneer organism to rigid and predictable organization. The work is begun by one person with a dream, who
risks all on that dream. As the dream takes shape, other people
attach themselves to that original dreamer and a movement
starts. Before long, an organized machine develops with de-
partments and charts and budgets and detailed job descrip-
tions. The next move is from machine to monument,
procedures are set in concrete, policies are unchangeable,
direction is unchallenged. The monument, as we know, is a
tomb. In the process, we have moved from high risk to safety
and certainty. And in the framework of machine or monument, nobody risks anything. We need all our resources just
to keep this behemoth going.

There's a profound lesson here for the church. A scene

in Gilbert and Sullivan's *Pirates of Penzance* points up all we've been saying. The hero, Frederick, having decided to try to capture those nasty pirates, enlists the aid of the police, who are typical "Keystone Kops." The police gather in the square while the women in the town sing "Go ye heroes, go to glory." And these "Keystone Kops" reply with endless choruses of "We go, we go, we go, we go." The general interrupts repeatedly to point out that they are not going anywhere. Nevertheless, they keep singing, "We go, we go, we go." The scene always reminds me of all the congregations I've been part of where we sing "Onward Christian Soldiers" lustily and nobody is going anyplace. Hearing God's call requires getting off your comfortable seat and moving out to the uncertain and the scary.

A Call with No Built-in Rewards

When Abraham arrives in the land of the Canaanites, God says to him, "To your descendants I will give this land," and apparently that is reward enough for Abraham. He is singularly unselfish. He is not working toward something he will ever personally own. Rather, he is acting in obedience to claim the promise that God has for those who will come after him. He is like a man who plants a forest of redwood trees. Quite often the absence of immediate success is the mark of a genuine call. Most of the heroes of the faith died with their dreams unfulfilled. Moses never got to the Promised Land. On the cross, Jesus Himself called out, "My God, my God, why hast Thou forsaken me?" He was not certain of the victory to come in just three days. The rewards of Abraham's obedience would be enjoyed by somebody else.

We can be comforted that the account in Genesis gives us a description of Abraham in all his humanity. He fails frequently. He lies, he is faithless. In Egypt he passes Sarah off as his sister, fearful that he will be killed should the Pharaoh desire her. His deceit is discovered when the Pharaoh tries to marry Sarah and finds she is already Abraham's wife. We'll talk about that in more detail later. But the point is, Abraham's call does not depend upon Abraham's faith in his own faithfulness. When he fails, he confesses his sins and keeps on trusting. He believes in the God who called him, not in himself and his own strength or faith.

But the quality I love, perhaps most of all, about Abraham is his perseverance. Abraham just kept on keeping on. He just kept on moving on as God seemed to lead. The secular historians tell us that was the genius of George Washington. They claim he was no military expert or intellectual genius but he had two qualities that insured the success of the American Revolution. He had integrity and perseverance. He just kept on in the face of all the defeats and setbacks until the revolution was won. As we respond to God's call today, we have no guarantee of success, but we persevere, saying, "God, you've called us to this work and we will not quit." We persevere as Job did, who said, "Though He slay me, yet will I trust Him."

God's Call Today

What, then, can we deduce about God's call to you and me today from this biblical account? First of all, we know that God initiates the call. It's a right-brain transaction. The call usually comes to busy people. You needn't take a week off to hear God's call. We tend to think that's so. "If I could just go off to a monastery or nunnery for a week, I might be able to hear God's call." This is not biblically sound. My friend Don Kea underscores this for us. He says, "Where (and when) does God's call come? God's call came to Moses when he was busy with his flock at Horeb. Gideon was busy threshing the wheat by the wine press. Saul was busy searching for his father's lost beasts and the call came. Elisha was busy plowing with twelve yoke of oxen. David was busy caring for his father's sheep. Nehemiah was busy bearing the king's wine cups. Amos was busy picking figs and caring for sheep. Peter and Andrew were busy casting nets into the sea. Lydia was busy preparing and buying and selling purple fabrics. James and John were busy mending their nets. Matthew was busy collecting taxes. Mary and Elizabeth were busy with their homemaking."

The call does not usually come to people with leisure. The call comes when you are busy about your work and it suddenly surprises you with its relentless urgency. Further, it is usually a specific call to a specific task to help some group of people somewhere, in a tangible way.

We have to say that Abraham's call was unique and unlike any other because God promised that as a result of his faithfulness every human being in the world would be blessed. He is, of course, the father of the Jewish nation, but ultimately from that nation came the Messiah, in whom there is, potentially, reconciliation and blessing for the whole world. While Abraham's call is unique, it is in another sense universal. God is still calling His people today. He hasn't changed. He is the same God yesterday and today and forever. He's still in the business of calling disciples to leave the certain and move out in trust and obedience.

Some years ago a young man named Martin Lloyd Jones was one of Britain's promising young surgeons. At age 23, he was the chief physician to the king. His diagnostic talents were remarkable. This young Welshman, the son of a dairy farmer, had been wrestling with a call to the ministry and had decided he could serve the Lord better as a Christian physician. One night, Martin Jones was leaving the theater with a friend and here, in his own words, is what happened to him: "As we came out of the theater, suddenly a Salvation Army band came along playing some hymn tunes. There is a theme in Wagner's opera *Tannhäuser* where there are two pulls—the pull of the world and the chorus of the pilgrims—and the contrast between the two. I know exactly what it means. When I heard this band and the hymns I said, 'These are my people. These are the people I belong to, and I'm going to belong to them.' " He left his medical practice and became the pastor of a tiny church in an impoverished Welsh mining town. His actions are illogical and unexplainable, apart from the call of God.

At this same time in Europe, a brilliant theologian named Albert Schweitzer was astounding the intellectual community. He held Ph.D.'s in many fields, including theology, music, medicine, and philosophy. As a matter of fact, he wrote a book called *A Quest for the Historical Jesus.* In the midst of all this worldly success, he heard God's call to be a medical missionary in a little rural village in southern Africa. At the height of his success, he renounced his career as a teacher of theology to serve a handful of people in a remote part of Africa, where he eventually died. Illogical and unexplainable.

More recently, God called a small-town country lawyer named Millard Fuller to do something about housing the world's poor. Half of the people in the world either have no place to live or dwell in miserable substandard housing. This young Georgia lawyer said, "We can change that." He began by going to Zaire, Africa, where he enlisted some help and built a few houses. His ministry is presently called Habitat for Humanity, and I have been on his advisory board from those beginning days. If you give money to Habitat for Humanity, it goes into a fund to buy a house. But the people who get that house eventually pay back the money interest-free. That seed money keeps on building more houses. Ultimately, if the Lord tarries, thousands of houses will be built with this revolving money supply. Millard says, "The poor don't need charity, they need capital." In ten years' time, through the initiative of one backwoods lawyer, homes have been built in fourteen overseas communities and thirty-three places in this nation. We need not wonder if God is calling people today.

Last year Sam Kamaleson, vice-president of World Vision

International, told some of us about a seventy-year-old lady in Melbourne who experienced a sudden and dramatic conversion. She went to her preacher and told him about her call to serve the Lord. What should she do? Unsure how to advise her, he suggested she go home and pray about it. She did that and the Lord seemed to give her a plan. She bought a batch of 3 x 5 cards and wrote on them, "Are you homesick? Come to my house for tea at 4," and she listed her address on the bottom. Next, she posted those little cards all around the University of Melbourne. For the next two weeks this little lady had tea ready at four o'clock every afternoon, but nobody came. At the end of that time, one Indonesian student showed up, homesick and as eager to talk as she was to listen, and together they drank tea. Back at the university, he told friends, "Guess what? I've met a lady just like my grandmother." Soon other students were coming. When she died ten years later, there were at least eighty pallbearers at her funeral—Indonesians, Indians, Pakistanis, and Malaysians. All of them had met the Lord because of the lady who served them tea every day at four o'clock.

Sometimes we cannot hear God's call because of our fear of the unfamiliar. A friend of mine is a Methodist minister in Columbus, Georgia, and he tells me that just before moving there, his twelve-year-old dog named Luv went blind as a result of cataracts. They worried about her adjustment to a new place but she did very well. She could smell her way around the backyard and the house and she was content. But one day, she went out and apparently wandered away. He finally found her down the street terrified, hugging the ground, trembling and shaking all over. She didn't know where she was. She was not in her familiar surroundings. My friend said, "I picked her up and brought her back and put her in the family room and immediately she knew where she was, and she could manage just fine."

A lot of us are like that old blind dog Luv. We're secure

because of familiar surroundings—church, job, friends, clubs, hobbies. We have a nice little routine in which we are comfortable. As long as we stay in that circle, we're secure and happy like old Luv and we'll never hear God's call. God asks us to leave all that. Not necessarily geographically, but to break the pattern and do new things that may be frightening. Instead of trusting in those secure patterns that we've built up over the years, we need to trust in God and test Him and know He is adequate.

I remember that at least once a year in my boyhood, my pastor read aloud Sidney Lanier's poem "The Marshes of Glynn." These are a few of my favorite lines:

> As the marsh-hen secretly builds on the watery sod
> Behold, I will build me a nest on the greatness of God:
> I will fly in the greatness of God as the marsh-hen flies
> In the freedom that fills all the space 'twixt the marsh and
>   the skies.
>
> By so many roots as the marsh-grass sends in the sod
> I will heartily lay me a-hold of the greatness of God:
> Oh, like to the greatness of God is the greatness within
> The range of the marshes, the liberal marshes of Glynn.

Are you building your nest on the greatness of God as Abraham did? The God who called him is calling us today to leave the familiar and to "go."

7. What Does God Want?

Genesis 12 and 13

Last Thanksgiving we experienced a day-long power outage. For the first time in thirty years, we ate no turkey and watched no televised football games. I found it's possible to be thankful, in spite of such handicaps. You sit in front of the fire and talk and play games and go back to basics. We discovered we still had all the things that really count, and we were thankful.

In the same vein, sometimes we need to strip our theology of all the nonessentials. It seems to me that all theology is concerned with two basic questions. First, Is there a God? Second, If there is, what does God want us to be and do? Those of us who are Christians have answered the first question affirmatively. God has given us the gift of faith. We know that He *is* or we wouldn't be worshiping and giving and serving and praying. The second question is the crucial one for us. What is it that God wants? It is at this point that heresy began with the first two human beings. Eve invented her own rules and ignored God's instructions. Our search, as we go through the book of Genesis, is to go back to the basics and try to find out what it is God wants.

We've been saying right along that the biblical narrative is largely right-brain language. It's like the pithy language of Madison Avenue. In that advertising world, tens of thousands of dollars are spent to make one thirty-second commer-cial which will put a picture in our minds of something we "can't live without." It's not logical that a thirty-second image or message should have such power to motivate us. In the twelfth and thirteenth chapters of Genesis we find two of these right-brain pictures side by side. The first communicates the wrong way to live and the second depicts a way of life that is pleasing to God.

A Cowardly Lie

In both stories, Abraham is the major figure. In the first story, the problem is famine. There is nothing to eat so Abraham and his company move south to Egypt which was at that time (and at the time of Joseph) the granary of the known world. But in Egypt there is a new danger—that the Egyptians will be attracted by Sarah's beauty and will kill Abraham to get her. In his desire to save himself, Abraham suggests a less than honorable solution. He asks Sarah to say she is his sister. Abraham plots to save himself with lies and deceit and perhaps, most reprehensible, by sacrificing Sarah. But his basic sin is that he lies and deceives because he does not trust God with his safety.

We were on the island of Skiathos in Greece on study leave a few years ago and we rented a house just down the beach from a luxury hotel built by the Greek government to attract tourists from all over northern Europe. On the grounds of this lovely hotel, with its beach and pools and restaurants, was an old, run-down farm, complete with smelly goats and noisy chickens. An old peasant couple lived there in a tumble-down shack. The wife did her laundry in a tub in the yard and put her clothes on the rocks to dry. All the tourists had to walk around this objectionable place to get from their hotel room to the beach. I asked our landlord how this had come about. He explained it this way, "When the builder offered to buy this man's land, he refused to sell. The builder threatened to get a government order that would force him to sell. The old peasant said, 'Fine, but on the day you bring that order, I plan to get out my service revolver and blow your brains out.' " Strangely enough, in Greece, tribal law supersedes federal law and the tribal law on that little island gives you license to kill anybody who takes your property. So, the farm continues to operate in the midst of the throngs of sun-bathing tourists. Apparently, tribal law in Pharaoh's Egypt dictated that all alien women were fair game and so Abraham devises this scheme to survive.

In this case, Abraham found a legal loophole to make it all sound legitimate. Sarah was actually his half-sister (Gen. 20:12). His treachery was discovered, however, by God's direct intervention. Pharaoh, who has taken Sarah for his wife and given Abraham many animals and servants in return, begins to suspect that something is wrong when plague hits his household. He says to Abraham, "What have you done to me? Here is your wife. Take her and be gone."

Grace and Graciousness

Have you ever been so ashamed you couldn't even defend yourself? Abraham could have said, "Well, you see, it wasn't really a lie because she's my half-sister." He attempts no defense. He's simply ashamed and guilty. Pharaoh, on the other hand, not only gives him a military escort out of the country, but allows him to keep all the gifts. He says, "Take them and get out of my sight." The embarrassing thing here is that the man of the world acts more honorably than the man of God. The man of God is discovered in his trickery and is ashamed, while the man of the world does the noble, gracious thing.

Have you ever been in that situation—embarrassed when your non-believing neighbors seem more generous, kind, and forgiving than you? I was downtown visiting with one of

our parishioners at his office recently and he gathered some
of his other Christian co-workers together for a brown bag
lunch. We were talking about witnessing in the office and
these people were a little chagrined that the manager of their
office, who is not a Christian, seems to be the finest person
around. He outcares and outloves most of them. How do
you witness to somebody like that? That raises the question
of what our witness is supposed to be about—that we are
the best people? Are we the new Pharisees, who say, "Isn't
it too bad that all the non-believers aren't like us?"

In *Christianity Today* Philip Yancey discusses this new Phari-
seeism. He reports that the Mormons spend a great deal of
money to sell their faith to the world. In a twelve-page ad
in *Reader's Digest* a few years ago, the tone of their message
was: "We are good people. We take care of our own. We
don't use alcohol, tobacco, coffee, tea, or caffeine of any kind.
We are kind and wonderful. Come and be like us." Unfortunately, you and I can't say that much of the time. What we
say is, "We believe there is a God who created us all and
who loves us all. As we listen to Him and follow His call,
we may stumble. But our witness is not that we are good
people. We are trying to be faithful to a living God. Come
join us."

This account in Genesis doesn't tell us what happened to
Pharaoh. Do he and his household ever get over the plague?
We don't know, for the story just ends there. Let's hope
that this charitable and forgiving man got well. In this picture
of the wrong way to live, Abraham tries to solve his problems
and save himself by trickery, but in the next story he behaves
quite differently.

Facing Choices

After leaving Egypt, Abraham continues to prosper and eventually both he and his nephew Lot are so rich that they have
become two huge households, too big to live together. When

they were poor they could be friends and neighbors, but prosperity changed all that. Abraham says to Lot, "Let there be no strife between you and me, and between your herdsmen and my herdsmen. . . . Is not the whole land before you? Separate yourself from me." And he leaves the choice to Lot. It's an especially strange proposal because neither of them actually owned any land. The land still belonged to the Canaanites and the Perizzites. These two families were simply allowed to graze their flocks over the fields after the harvest. The landowners gave them permission to do so, or perhaps they paid for grazing privileges. We don't know. The point is, they owned nothing, but they decided to go different ways lest they face more problems, more fighting, and possibly even death.

This is one of Abraham's finest moments. Instead of looking out for his own interests, as he did in Egypt, he lets Lot do the choosing. His nephew can have whatever he wants. "If you take the left hand, I'll go right. If you take the right hand, I'll go left," says Abraham. You'd think that fine young man would have said, "Well, Uncle Abe, you're the senior and I'm the junior; you're the organizer and leader of this whole expedition. I'll take the high, barren ground and give you the lush valley of the Jordan with its water and fertile fields." Instead, he says, "My choice? I'll take the best land."

The story reminds me of the little boy who was asked by his Sunday school teacher, "Now, if you had two apples, John, a great big red one and a small wormy one, and you were told to give one to your brother, which one would you give him?" Pondering the problem a moment, Johnny asked, "My older brother or my younger one?" Somebody has said that we all favor an equal distribution of the wealth as long as we get more than we started with. Lot's choice here is the human one. Given his choice, of course, he'll take the best portion. As soon as Abraham in faith lets the inferior, the younger, have his choice, God gives him His promise of favor—that all the land he could see, north, south, east, and west, will belong to him and to his descendants. In giving Lot the choice, Abraham acted in faith, and God honored him for that.

It's better to be an Abraham, moving out and trying to be obedient to God and occasionally failing, than to be morally perfect in some safe harbor. God wants obedience on the journey. You will fail and that's where God's grace comes in and rescues you. Sarah was rescued from Pharaoh's household. God did not act in order to spare Abraham humiliation. Sarah was an important part of His plan. She was to be the mother of the Jewish race and beyond that, an ancestor of the Messiah. Out of her lineage would come the child that was to bless the whole world. God spared both Sarah and Abraham for His own purposes.

What then does God want? He wants us to believe He is our friend, to trust Him, to trust His overall purpose, His power, His goodness, and His reliability. When you get yourself into a horrendous mess, you may try to save yourself by the kind of trickery, conniving, and maneuvering that Abraham practiced with Pharaoh. But if we can admit before the church and the world that we blew it and say, "God help me," He can deliver us.

A friend and fellow pastor, Art Sueltz, told about a man he knew who bought a lovely house in the suburbs. On the day he moved in, the man's new neighbor came running across the yard in an obviously belligerent state. "Did you buy this house?" asked the neighbor. "Yes, I did," was the reply. The neighbor continued, "Well, I want to tell you something. You bought a lawsuit. You see that fence of yours? It's at least seven feet over on my side of the line, and if it takes every dollar I've got, I intend to sue you and get that fence moved." The new homeowner said, "Well, neighbor, I'm sorry to hear this. I bought this house in good faith, but I believe you're telling the truth about this situation and I'll tell you what I'm going to do. First thing tomorrow morning, I'll have that fence moved back those seven feet." The neighbor was dumbfounded. "What did you say?" The new owner repeated, "I'm going to have that fence moved back seven feet." "No, you're not," was the response. "You leave it right where it is, and anything else you need is yours for the asking."

Sometimes when we leave the choice to the other person, miracles happen, but that didn't work for Abraham. He gave Lot his choice and Lot took advantage of him. There is no gimmick here that by preferring the other person you'll be blessed. But it is an attitude that often knocks the props out from under the average citizen.

The Royal Law

What does God want? He wants us to trust Him and to practice the royal law which is to prefer one another in love. It is the law modeled for us by Jesus who is equal with God, who made the world, and who left all that power and majesty to come to earth as a humble servant, born of a peasant to serve and heal us. Ultimately, He allowed us to kill Him. His message to us is, "Love one another as I have loved you. Greater love has no man than this, that a man lay down his life for his friends" (John 15:12–13). This is the royal law the King Himself has modeled for us. Thousands of years before the Messiah came, Abraham understood this kind of royal law. He gave up his own rights and preferred lot, and God blessed him mightily as a result of that act.

These two short chapters of Genesis show us two contrasting ways to live life. We can take care of ourselves by conniving and deceiving or just by clever maneuvering or we can practice the royal law, preferring one another in love.

Whenever I pass a certain chain of hamburger emporiums or hear their commercials on television, it's a reminder to me of this royal law. "Have it your way" is their slogan. That's what God would have us say in everyday situations because we trust Him. We can say to our spouse, our children, our parents, our boss, our secretary, our colleagues—whoever—"Have it your way." It's an alien concept for most of the world. What are some of the recent best-selling books? *Looking Out for Number One,* which sold millions of copies. *Winning through Intimidation,* whose message is "Take care of yourself. Don't let those buzzards grind you down." God expects something totally different. He says, "Don't take care of yourself. Prefer one another and trust in me."

Gert Behanna, who wrote *The Late Liz,* was an amazing character. She was converted at age 60 and became one of the great evangelists of our time, speaking to groups all over the country. She told me this story: "You know I travel around speaking for God and in the process I'm forced to use gas station restrooms which are almost always filthy. I used to complain about that to God. I'd say, 'Lord, if I'm your servant, how come I've got to use these dirty restrooms?' One day in the midst of this kind of complaint, He seemed to say, 'Gert, I come into this restroom too, right after you.' Somehow, I'd never thought about that." From that moment on, she said she never left a public restroom without cleaning the mirror, wiping out the sink and picking towels up off the floor. After all that, she'd say, "There You are, Lord. I hope it's clean enough for You." Thereafter, instead of bemoaning the mess she found, she began to prefer the next person coming in. It's a whole different way to live. Most of us would settle for taking the manager to task. It would not occur to us to take responsibility for the situation and try to improve it.

A Realistic Approach

In applying this royal law, it seems we need to keep a few things in mind. First, we don't do it because we believe in the innate goodness of the other person. The failure of communism, basically, is the assumption that once we get the capitalists off the backs of the working classes, we'll all love one another and work together for the common good. We Calvinists don't believe that people are naturally good and other-directed. We believe in original sin and total depravity. We prefer one another as an act of faith in God, not because we believe in the goodness of man.

Next, we do not prefer the other person for thanks or rewards. I live in a sizable city and I am stopped frequently by people asking for five dollars (or fifty dollars). They say, "I've never asked anybody before. I'll mail it back to you as soon as I get to my destination. I just need enough gas to take me there." I've handed out a lot of five dollar bills and I have yet to have anybody write and say, "Thank you. Here's your money back." Every time I help someone in this way, I am reasonably certain, on the basis of experience, that this is a con game. Why do I do it? As an act of faith in God. When our daughter began work as an attorney in legal services, one of the first things she had to struggle with was the lack of gratitude on the part of her clients, in this case poor migrant farm workers. Since these people get free legal services, paid for by tax dollars, you might expect them to be overwhelmed with gratitude and eager to cooperate. They're not. They show up late, miss appointments, and complain about the progress of their case. As we live out the royal law, most people are not going to say, "Aren't you wonderful!" They'll take advantage of you as Lot took advantage of Abraham.

We're not to prefer one another in love because we are fearful of a contest. God doesn't want us to be wimps or doormats. If you give in to people because you're frightened, there is no blessing in that. Abraham was stronger than Lot. When warfare raged in Sodom and Lot was taken captive, it was Abraham who, with just 318 men, put the enemy armies to rout and rescued Lot.

Finally, our faith in God must be demonstrated to our brother. How can we say we love God whom we've not seen if we can't love our brother, whom we have seen?

(1 John 4:20). If we love God, we must act out that love
to our brothers and sisters. For example, in marriage, the
harder I push my wife over some issue, the more defensive
she gets. When one party backs off, we both become more
open to reason. It's a truth that applies to parents and children,
labor and management. The more we push for advantage,
the more the other resists. When you begin to live God's
way, as I've discovered all too infrequently in my life, we
can reverse those natural tendencies to compete and to win.
We can say to the other person, "Have it your way." That
may be exactly what God wants.

8. When You Least Expect It

Genesis 14

I wonder what you thought of when you saw this chapter's title? When you least expect it, what happens? Disaster hits! A lot of us live by Murphy's Law. "If anything can possibly go wrong, it will." When you least expect it—the bottom falls out, the roof caves in, catastrophe strikes.

Actually, what I had in mind was that when we least expect it, God has something good for us. He does for Abraham in the fourteenth chapter of Genesis. God surprises him with a priest who comes from nowhere, blesses him, and is never seen or heard from again. We've been talking about believing that God is our friend and, as proof of that friendship, He wants to give good gifts to you and me. In return, He wants to receive our love and friendship. We are to give and receive from each other. God initiates this giving and receiving.

Believing the Best

A lot of us Christians love to give, but we may tend to be stingy receivers. We're programmed for giving and serving, but we're not programmed to expect much back. And that's especially unfortunate because, for the most part, what we expect we get. Some of us have a faculty for expecting the best even when the worst happens. Last year, our church

79

business manager was pulled over by the police on suspicion of drunk driving. He was on his way to a meeting of church business managers, a group for which he is the regional president. He was stopped by a female state trooper and her colleague and they observed that he seemed to want to monopolize both lanes of the highway. Allan tried to explain, "I'm not drunk. In fact, I'm a teetotaler. But, I'm very tired and I think I started to fall asleep." "In that case, you need help," was the response. "There's a restaurant down the road where you can get coffee, or pull over in the next rest area and take a nap." He took their advice and got to his meeting safely.

Returning the next day, he decided to stop at the police barracks and look up the trooper and thank her. "I think you might be an angel God sent to save my life last night." I'm sure that was the first time she'd ever been called that. But Allan is the kind of guy who believes that God has good things for him even when he is stopped by the police.

Some years ago, Hazel and I were leading a tour to the Holy Land which included a Mediterranean cruise. The ship stopped in Yugoslavia at Dubrovnik. All 500 passengers went ashore to see this wonderful medieval city. Back on board after the shore excursion, we numbered only 498. Two passengers were missing—our daughter and her roommate. This was especially serious in a communist country. The ship cannot leave unless everyone is aboard. (They don't want any CIA agents left behind!) I hailed a cab to go to town and look for the two girls, accompanied by the ship's first mate.

As we drove along, I shared my anxieties. "I know something terrible has happened to them. These are two sophisticated, knowledgeable young women. One's a lawyer and one's a banker. They are responsible and intelligent. They would be here unless something awful has happened. They were either kidnapped by white slavers or they're in a hospital. I just know it." Now, the first mate of the *S. S. Victoria,* not knowing that he was talking to a man of faith, turned and gave me some words of wisdom. He said, "Mister, let me give you a rule to live by the rest of your life. 'Always expect the best first.' " Not bad advice.

We didn't find the girls but by the time we got back to the ship, they had already returned. They had simply gotten the sailing time confused. But I was expecting the worst as though God did not intend good things for us.

It's like the story about the policeman who came upon a circle of people trying to revive an elderly woman lying prone in the street in front of a car. "Who's the driver of this car?" asked the policeman. A man stepped forward. "I am." "How did you hit her?" the policeman asked. "I didn't hit her," was the reply. "I was turning the corner and I stopped to let her cross the street and she fainted." Like that lady, a lot of us are just not programmed to believe that drivers are going to stop and let pedestrians cross the street. We're programmed to expect them to run us down.

A Rescue Expedition

As we pick up the story of Abraham and Sarah, warfare on an international scale is raging all around them. Like us, Abraham and Sarah have to live out their faith in the real world. We can't go off someplace where we're assured of quiet and safety. Then and now, there are wars and rumors of wars. Lot, having settled in Sodom, is captured when Sodom and Gomorrah are overrun by enemy forces. This news reaches Abraham and he sets off to rescue his kinsman. Somebody has said, "Many people are saved from sin because they are so inept at it." I think Lot must have been like that. He's neither strong nor clever. He chooses the best portion and finds himself a victim and a prisoner of enemy kingdoms.

Poor old Uncle Abe must come to the rescue. He does so with just 318 men against a coalition of five kings and their armies, and he brings back not only Lot but his goods and the women and the whole company. We're not told in

detail how he accomplished this but it's the kind of story
we find on many later occasions in the Old Testament. Gideon, with a few hundred men, conquered thousands. David,
while still a teenager, took on the biggest and the toughest
man around and defeated him. Over and over again, the
little and the few on God's side win out against the mighty
and powerful. Abraham lived grace. He received God's forgiveness for his chicanery in Egypt and he holds no grudge
against Lot. He might have said, "Lot captured? Too bad.
He made his bed; let him lie in it." Instead, he leads his
trained men out against Lot's captors and rescues him.

A doctor friend recently gave me a copy of a report by
a group of researchers headed by Dr. Redford B. Williams
of Duke University Medical School. They have collected a
lot of evidence to indicate that it is not Type A (compulsive,
workaholic) behavior that is a leading cause of death in our
modern society, but hostility. The root cause of illness, they
are saying, lies somewhere in the neuroendocrine response
of angry people. It doesn't matter whether you repress your
anger or express it. If you are hostile, apparently, your body
responds negatively and illness results. To live by grace means
forgiving yourself and forgiving the people who offend you,
simply because God has forgiven you.

The Unexpected Gift

Having defeated these five kings, Abraham returns home
with Lot and his whole company and all the booty and he
is surprised by joy. God has a gift for him. Out of nowhere
a mysterious figure appears—Melchizedek, king of Salem.
(I think it's interesting that Salem, which means "peace," is
part of the name for Jerusalem.) Melchizedek blesses Abraham and affirms that God is pleased with him. They have
wine and bread together, a pre-communion ritual. Abraham
offers Melchizedek a tithe, a tenth of all the spoils, an indication that this man who has no antecedent or precedent is a

significant figure. (The Book of Hebrews mentions Melchize-dek as a type of the Christ, an early forerunner of our Lord Jesus who is our High Priest in the New Covenant.)

That sort of unexplainable serendipity still happens. Un-planned and out of nowhere, God may send a mysterious figure to bless us. At brunch one day, a lady in our congrega-tion, Maudine, told Hazel and me an interesting story. During the Christmas holidays, she attended the funeral of a dear friend. She was sad about the death of course, but she was also depressed by the funeral service where Jesus was never mentioned and no word of hope was offered. Back home that night, she couldn't seem to shake the blues and she de-cided to do something about it. She would go downtown to a local department store and mingle with the holiday shop-pers.

She was browsing in the picture frame department when she noticed a woman looking for a special frame to give a friend as a Christmas gift. It seems she had found just the right one but the price was more than she could afford. She discussed the matter briefly with the clerk and then walked away looking sorrowful. At that point, a couple standing near Maudine said to the saleslady, "We'd like to buy that frame for her. Put it on our account. But don't tell her who paid for it." Immediately, the clerk ran after her customer. "Par-don me, but you own this frame. Someone has bought it for you." The woman began to cry, the clerk began to cry, my friend Maudine began to cry, everybody was crying be-cause of this unexpected act of generosity.

When you are depressed, where do you go? I suggest that you go downtown or to a shopping mall. That may just prove to be more therapeutic than your private prayer room. God is where the action is. Where do you find angels? Sometimes in Frederick and Nelson's Department Store in Seattle. Think of it. You can be a Melchizedek for the price of one picture frame. That's all it takes.

All of us live in the real world where we are called on

to live out our faith in some hard places. Frank Tillapaugh, author and pastor, in speaking to a group of Seattle pastors last year, said that one problem with the church today is that we've inherited a rural mentality which leads to false expectations. The church in America began and flourished on the frontier in small towns where there was at least a superficial harmony. In our large cities, it would seem that the best we can hope for is conflict management. With so many interests represented, harmony is not even a possibility. Most of us live in urban areas where conflict rather than harmony is the norm. In that real world, let God surprise you. Expect Him to do so when you least expect it—on a bad day when you've blown it fifteen times. That's when some Melchizedek may walk into your life, some angel on the highway, some unknown donor in a department store, somebody to say, "I've got something good for you."

I was writing and outlining this chapter during my study leave last summer on Whidbey Island off the Washington coast, and as I wrote the words "Expect God to surprise you with good things," I looked out the window and there, for the first time in my life, I saw a pod of six black and white killer whales go by just off the beach. One of them actually leaped clear out of the water. I couldn't believe what I was seeing. Then I realized that was the very thing I was writing about. It's as though God were saying, "Larson, you're on the right track. Expect good things."

Does it seem puzzling that somebody named Larson ended up in a Presbyterian church? It's a strange story. I ought to be a Swedish Covenanter or a Lutheran. It's all because one day, a few years before I was born, my father was driving down Michigan Boulevard in Chicago in a driving rain. He saw a man waiting for a bus and he pulled over to offer him a ride. The man accepted with pleasure. In the course of the drive, the man asked, "What church do you go to?" "I don't go to church. I'm a free thinker," said my dad. "Well, I'm John Timothy Stone, pastor of the Fourth Presbyterian Church," said the passenger. "Here is my card. I want to see you in church on Sunday. Give this to an usher and he'll give you a good seat. Come up and talk to me after the service." My father not only went, but he eventually joined that church and later became a deacon. Even later, he became a Christian. That's how I happen to be a Presbyterian. My father was a Melchizedek to a stranger standing in the rain. And that man turned out to be a Melchizedek to him, a great soul winner who sought out individuals one by one and asked, "Are you a Christian? If not, why not?"

Contemporary Melchizedeks

We have the same opportunity to be an unexpected blessing to others when they least expect it. You can be a Melchizedek, a mysterious stranger coming from nowhere who brings God's blessing. My roommate in college had a Melchizedek in his life. Wally was the son of an impoverished Methodist minister and when he felt the call to go into the ministry after college, an unknown patron paid his tuition. Wally never knew exactly where the money came from but this affluent businessman had heard about him and wanted to sponsor him. The government was my benefactor and put me through seminary on the GI Bill, but my friend had a more personal Melchizedek.

Being a Melchizedek does not necessarily have to involve money. You can simply be someone who tells people who are doing a good job that you appreciate them. Be an affirmer. There are never enough of those around. Mark Twain once said, "I can live two weeks on one good compliment." I can too. I have told my own congregation many times that it takes ten "atta-boys" to equal one "you jerk." We need those appreciators who say, "Atta-boy, keep on going." This past year I had a letter from a couple who wrote, "We've been around the church now as long as you have—almost four years—and we appreciate you. We've never told you

before. We might not write again for four years, but, nevertheless, know that every week we appreciate you." I'm saving
that letter. On bad days I'll get it out and re-read it and
remember that somebody appreciates me.

Over the last few years, our church has witnessed the phe-
nomenal growth of a Cambodian congregation under our
sponsorship. It is the largest Cambodian Christian church in
the world outside of a refugee camp. We are the unexpected
hosts for this group because five or six years ago some couples
in our church decided to be Melchizedeks to a few Cambodian
refugee families. They found them places to live, scavenged
for used furniture and household things, and lined up language instructors. From that tiny start, more and more members of the congregation became involved and now we're
embarrassed by the riches that God has given to us through
this exciting Cambodian church.

A few years ago I was the week-long chaplain at Chautau-
qua, the famous old New York state conference grounds
near Jamestown. Dr. Karl Menninger was there that same
week and he was celebrating his eighty-seventh birthday. He
read this column on that occasion. He is not the author of
it, but it expressed his philosophy:

> People are unreasonable, illogical and self-centered: love them
> anyway.
> If you do good, people will accuse you of selfish ulterior motives:
> do good anyway.
> If you're successful, you win false friends and make true enemies:
> try to succeed anyway.
> The good you do today will be forgotten tomorrow: be good
> anyway.
> Honesty and frankness will get you nowhere: They make you
> vulnerable. Be honest and frank anyway.
> People favor underdogs, but they follow the top dogs: fight
> for some underdogs anyway.
> What you spend days building may be destroyed overnight: do
> it anyway.

People really need help but they attack you if you try to help
them: try anyway.
Give the world the best you have and you get kicked in the
mouth: give the world the best you have anyway.

That's pretty good advice from one of our pioneer psychia-
trists. It's the philosophy that Abraham practiced. However
undeserving Lot was, Abraham risked his life for him, rescued
him from slavery, and saved him from possible death. On
the homeward journey, God meets him through this remarkable priest Melchizedek who serves him bread and wine and
who blesses him.

Expecting the Unexpected

A friend of mine lost her husband two years ago after many
years of happy marriage. She's been an example to me of
how to handle grief. Recently, she wrote me: "This has been
for me a confusing time. You know how deeply I loved my
husband and expected that he would be the one love of my
life. But now I find that God has brought someone along
who makes me feel alive again. This kind of emotion is hard
on an old gal of sixty-six, you may be sure." Does God want
to surprise an old gal of sixty-six? I believe He does. And I
think there's a wonderful surprise for the guy in her life as
well. When you lose your life's partner, you may be prepared
to be a widow or widower until the day of your death. When
you least expect it, God may have something better for you.

A couple I know were driving down the freeway a few
months ago and they saw a young hitchhiker carrying a big
sign. The sign said, "Rides now being accepted." It did *not*
say, "Won't you please pick me up? I'm going to Portland."
The young man was expecting good things. His sign implied
he would consider your offer.

A story appeared in the *Denver Post* last year that sums
up what we've been saying. A week or so before Christmas,

a pastor told his congregation about a needy family who, because of the recession and some other problems, were facing a very bleak Christmas. One young father decided to do something about that. He and his son set out in the family pickup truck to cut down a fresh evergreen and deliver it to this destitute family. They ran into a rockslide and a boulder hit the truck. It was totally destroyed. The windshield was smashed and while the father was not hurt, the young boy was cut by the glass and was bleeding severely. They tried to wave down a passing motorist to help, but to no avail. Finally, after over two hundred cars had whizzed by, one stopped. The couple in the car took care of the injured boy, returned the two of them to their home, and then went on. The father and son never got the names of their two Melchizedeks.

In a week's time the truck was repaired and the boy's injury healed. On Christmas Eve, the pastor asked this same man if he would deliver a basket of food and toys to the needy family he had set out to bring the tree to earlier on. He was glad to. They loaded up the truck and drove to the address they were given and rang the doorbell. Who should answer the door but the couple who had stopped to help him on the highway just weeks before. They proved to be Melchizedeks to each other.

Our Creator's nature is to give us good gifts and we are to pass those blessings on as fast as we get them. Expect God to send people into your life to bless you. Don't be a stingy receiver. When you least expect it, look for a blessing or try to be one.

At the same time, let's keep in mind that any relationship of love depends not on the giving of gifts but on the giving of self. God's supreme gift is Himself and His friendship, and friendship is the gift He most desires to receive from us.

9. God Wants Friends

Genesis 15

The Bible speaks often of "the word of the Lord." Perhaps you've wondered exactly what "the word" refers to and what "the word of the Lord" means. In Scotland, there is a cultural definition of "the word." When some miner is lost in a cave-in, some sailor perishes at sea, or some young mother dies in childbirth, the question is, "Who will bring the word?" The "word" is synonymous with bad news that must be broken to family and friends.

But "the word of the Lord" ought to be good news and its meaning self-evident. If the wind and fire of the Spirit are to be released in and through God's people, we need first of all to go back to allowing the Bible to explain itself. Most of us approach the Bible with our own grid of spirituality or piety or theological emphasis. We interpret the word in the context of our bias. When we let the word (the Bible) explain itself, we find the message is better and more powerful and more efficacious than we ever dared dream.

In the first verse of chapter 15, the word of the Lord comes to Abraham to reassure and comfort him. God gives Abraham a powerful word and that word is that he is to *trust.* In verses 2 and 3, Abraham immediately begins to complain and doubt. He prays a whining prayer, as I have done all too often. We might paraphrase it this way. "O Lord, I have a serious problem. I know You led me out of Ur of the Chaldees and You delivered me in Egypt when I could have been killed. Pharaoh made me rich and I've prospered even more since then. But what have You done for me lately? The problem that keeps me awake at night is that I have no heir. You've made me rich and I'm going to die and who's going to get all these riches? Eliezer, a slave in my household?" (That was the law of the time: If you were childless, your senior slave became your heir.)

Examining Our Anxieties

I suggest that this prayer is like a mirror reflecting for us Abraham's underlying anxiety about life. This father of the faithful, like you and me, had frequent and recurring anxieties. If all our Bible study focuses on "What does God say?" and we never talk to Him about our own underlying anxieties, we miss one whole dimension of the dialogue God wants to initiate. We are frail, broken people. It's part of the human condition. In this chapter, Abraham is sharing his anxieties with God.

I belong to a Bible study and prayer support group, and we meet every Tuesday at 7:00 A.M. Last summer, we felt we needed more time to get to know each other better and, consequently, we set aside a whole day to be together. As we wrestled with the question of how best to use that time, we decided to begin the day with this question: What is it you fear more than death, or in other words, what is your underlying anxiety about life? Amazingly, no two of us had the same anxieties. Finding out that we were definitely God's Cabbage Patch dolls—all different—was a breakthrough in getting to know each other. If I know what terrifies you and you know the things I dread most, we can better pray for and support each other.

The story of John Knox, one of our great reformer heroes in Scotland, is a remarkable one. He was not converted until he was forty years of age. By means of a powerful preacher, "the word of the Lord" came to John Knox and he decided to be a preacher. At forty-one he was chaplain to the soldiers at Edinburgh Castle. At forty-two, Knox was captured as Britain was overrun by the French. He was sent to work on a French galley where he was chained to a bench and pulling an oar. It's not hard to imagine some of his underlying anxieties. "Lord, at forty I heard your word and said yes. At forty-one, I was called to preach and now, one year later, I'm reduced to pulling this dumb oar and I may never get out of this galley alive." That was certainly a possibility. But just nineteen months later, he was returned home and took up preaching anew, fearlessly proclaiming God's word to Scotland and to the whole world. But those nineteen months in the galley must have produced a lot of underlying anxieties. It must have been difficult to go on trusting and loving God.

True wisdom includes some understanding of self, of one's own fears and weaknesses. A lot of us are not all that eager to look at what's inside and deal with it. John Calvin once confessed, "I have not so great a struggle with my vices, numerous as they are, as I have with my impatience. My efforts are not absolutely useless, yet I've never been able to conquer this wild beast." Perhaps, for Calvin, impatience was his worst sin. He no doubt had all the garden variety of sins that you and I have. But his impatience implied a lack of trust. That's true for a lot of us. Thomas Carlyle shared this same sort of underlying anxiety. He said, "I have a natural talent for being in a hurry, which is a very bad talent."

By contrast, we read about Susannah Wesley, mother of the John Wesley who founded the Methodist Church. Susannah had twelve living children and still found time to be their spiritual mentor, taking time with each one every day. John recalls hearing his father say to his mother on one occasion, "Dear, why do you tell that dunderhead John the same thing twenty times? You're wasting your time." "No, dear," she corrected him. "If I told him only nineteen times I'd be wasting my time."

Perhaps your anxiety stems more from procrastination than from impatience. Procrastination is often blamed on laziness, but I think that's not usually the case. Often, we postpone some project because we are not certain of success. Our real problem is our fear of failure. Anxiety has as many causes and forms as there are people, but Abraham knew clearly the source of his and he's complaining that God ought to do something about this childless situation.

Trusting God's Plan

In response, God promises Abraham that his descendants will be as numerous as the stars in the sky. Abraham believed the Lord and it was "reckoned to him as righteousness." When his certainty begins to fade, the Lord makes a covenant with him by means of a sacrificial offering. Abraham puts three animals and two birds on the altar and when darkness falls, the offering is mysteriously burned. It is a dramatic covenant and Abraham doubts no more.

However, in the sixteenth chapter, Sarah comes along with an alternate plan—Plan B, if you will. She's not sure that God knows what He's about or that He understands human limitations. She concocts a scheme to help God out. Since she's too old to bear children, she suggests Abraham have a child with her maid, Hagar, a child they can raise as their own. That's called a contingency plan. And Abraham approved of the idea. In those days, such a course was perfectly legal. Your wife's maids were available to you sexually. Ishmael was the issue of this union of Abraham with Hagar—Ishmael, the father of the Arab world.

But the story, most of all, indicates that Abraham and Sarah have stopped trusting. They doubt that God will do as He said and give them an heir and they devise this scheme to help Him out. A member of our church gave me a poem I love. The author is unknown.

> As children bring their broken toys with tears for us to mend,
> I brought my broken dreams to God because He was my
>   friend.

But, then instead of leaving Him in peace to work alone,
I hung around and tried to help in ways that were my own.
At last I snatched them back and cried, "How can you be
  so slow?"
"My child," He said, "You never let them go."

That's what Abraham and Sarah did. They took their destiny
into their own hands because they didn't believe that God
was able to keep His promises.

In chapter 17, God appears again to Abraham. By this
time he is ninety-nine years old. When God promises Abraham that he will have a son with Sarah, this great man of
faith starts to laugh. In fact, he rolls on the ground laughing.
His response to God's promise this time is uncontrollable
mirth. Does God really understand the facts of life? Abraham
suggests to God that they forget about a son by Sarah and
settle for Ishmael. God agrees to bless Ishmael, but He promises that the covenant will be with Isaac, the son who will
be born to Abraham and Sarah. God does not let Abraham
settle for less than His best plan.

The story continues in chapter 18, with Abraham and Sarah
sitting in front of their tent at high noon on a very hot day.
Three strange visitors arrive, one of whom is the Lord. Abraham rushes out and kills a calf, and he and Sarah make some
cakes and serve them to the guests with true Middle Eastern
hospitality. When they have eaten, the one who is the Lord
says to Abraham, "Sarah, your wife, shall have a son." Sarah,
who's listening inside the tent, hears this and begins to laugh.
The Lord asks why she is laughing and she denies she has
done so. She is fearful and tries to disguise her unbelief.

A Trustworthy Friend

The whole story is an astonishing one and in it we find two
powerful truths. First of all, righteousness is defined for us

once and for all. We need not bring our definition of righteousness to the word. The word of God tells us what God considers righteousness to be. Genesis 15:6 says, "He believed the Lord, and he reckoned it to him as righteousness." In the New Testament, James quotes this very verse and completes it: "Abraham believed God, and it was reckoned to him as righteousness, and he was called the friend of God" (James 2:23). I could have entitled this chapter "God Demands Righteousness" and perhaps that's a truth those of us in the conservative tradition feel more at home with. We know God *does* demand righteousness, but, by God's own definition here, righteousness is believing and trusting in Him—believing He is your friend and trusting that He wants good things for you.

We can tell the world that God demands righteousness, or we can say that God wants friends, friends who'll believe and trust Him. Righteousness is not moral perfection. Marriage is a relationship of trust, but we do not expect perfection in our mate. Who has a perfect marriage? We cannot say, "Listen, I'm planning to marry you and from now on I will never fail you. I will never disappoint you. I'll never let you down." It's not possible to make that kind of promise. But we can keep our marriage vows in spite of our relational or moral imperfection. It is possible to say, "I'm committed to you, no matter what."

Righteousness in Abraham's case was trusting God even when He was silent. God made promises and years passed before they were realized. How much we all need to learn to trust God in the silences, to trust Him when we fail Him and when we doubt. Even in those times, we don't go back to Ur of the Chaldees. We stay in the place God has given us whether we've had a great day or a rotten one, whether we've believed or doubted. We live out our faith in a God who will do what He has promised, in spite of our weakness or our failures.

Pursuing Righteousness

The second message we find in this particular word of the Lord is that righteousness is attainable. Not human righteousness, of course. Not the righteousness that comes through the law. Even if you and I could keep perfectly the Ten Commandments and live out all the Beatitudes, which of course we can't, that wouldn't be enough. We would still be, at heart, sinners who "fall short of the glory of God" (Romans 3:23). Human righteousness is like filthy rags and God is not in the dirty laundry business. He's in the redemption business. The righteousness we can attain is the gift of God to believe He can do what He says He will, even when we don't believe. He can handle our unbelief as He did Abraham's and Sarah's.

Too often we get caught up instead in legalism which does not allow for failure. The transactional analysis people, who have given us so many good insights, say that most of us have tapes playing inside of us telling us how to perform. The tapes are usually admonitions from parents during our formative years—phrases like: "Be strong!" "Don't cry!" "Please other people!" "Try harder!" "Be perfect!"

We keep whipping ourselves into shape because failure is unthinkable. But these are not biblical injunctions. God's people, according to the biblical record, fail constantly and yet they keep on trusting.

It's sometimes especially hard to trust that God is at work in other people's lives. A lot of us fall into the trap of wanting to see results as we attempt to be God's instrument to affect and influence someone else. Last Christmas, one of the deacons in our congregation told me she would not be with her church family for the Christmas Eve services for the first time in many years. I asked why. "I'm baking a turkey and a ham and I'm taking that, along with some crackers and cheese, down to First Avenue" (an area in our city full of indigents and street people). "Did you know," she continued, "that every year the highest suicide rate in Seattle is on Christmas Eve around First Avenue? A group of us are going down there to put on a party for anybody who wants to come." I said, "Maybe we should all abandon our candlelight services and go with you." Now my friend had no guarantee that her going would actually help anyone, but she planned to be there anyway with a turkey and a ham and love and leave the results to God.

We Christians have made much of the verse, "The fear of the Lord is the beginning of wisdom." That's been corrupted to mean that we serve the Lord because we're afraid of punishment. In any love relationship, some degree of fear is always present. We are afraid we will do something that will embarrass or alienate the person we love. I have a very real fear of failing God and my family and those I love most. My fear is that I will not be all that I can be. That kind of fear is a natural part of the love relationship. But the relationship, basically, is one of trust. Even when God is silent, trust Him. Even when we don't believe, trust Him. Even when we are disobedient, trust Him. Abraham did.

Waiting for the Tide

In Europe and some of our northeastern seaport cities, there are enormous tides. I've seen them, especially on the west coast of England and Wales. In some of those great harbors when the tide is out, all sorts of vessels are lying inert in the mud banks, from huge ships to tiny fishing boats. You can scarcely see the sea. You wonder how these ships will ever reach water again. But, if you wait a few hours, the tide comes in, inexorably, silently, and raises those ships once again and they are free to sail on. There's no evidence that will happen while they are lying on the mud flats. When God seems silent and we begin to doubt, can you and I believe that the tide of His love will come in once more and raise us? You're a friend of God if you can trust Him when the tide is out, certain it will eventually come in again.

A few years ago a young man in our parish told me the moving story of his childhood. At the time of his birth, his father abandoned both his mother and him. A few years later, his mother left him in an orphanage—double abandonment. While he was still very young, his mother remarried and took him out of the orphanage, but, before long, she left both her new husband and her son. At that point, the story takes a happier turn. That new stepfather said to this twice-abandoned little boy, "I want to keep you. I want to raise you as my son." The tide was out a very long time for my friend. Eventually, it came in through his stepfather, who loved him and claimed him as his own.

In Jeremiah, God says, "For I know the plans I have for you, plans for welfare and not calamity, to give you a future and a hope." God may be silent now. The tide may be out. But we can believe that God has good plans for us and that is our hope for the future. In *The Fellowship of the Ring,* J. R. R. Tolkien gives us this poem:

> All that is gold does not glitter,
>   Not all those who wander are lost;
> The old that is strong does not wither,
>   Deep roots are not reached by the frost.
> From the ashes a fire shall be woken,
>   A light from the shadows shall spring;
> Renewed shall be blade that was broken,
>   The crownless again shall be king.*

The key verse of these four great chapters of Genesis is 18:14, where God asks the question, "Is anything too hard for the Lord?" If we can believe that nothing is, then we have the gift of faith. This is what makes us righteous and, like Abraham, we become a friend of God—and He wants friends.

---

* From *The Fellowship of the Ring* by J. R. R. Tolkien. Copyright © 1965 by J. R. R. Tolkien. Reprinted by permission of Houghton Mifflin Company, and by George Allen & Unwin, Ltd.

10. Sin, Sodom, and Survival

Genesis 18 and 19

On the first day of the new year, many of us make formal or informal resolutions about things we'd like to change in our lives. The making of such resolutions presupposes some kind of a value system. We have pretty clear ideas about what is good and beneficial and what is harmful and destructive, what is good and what is evil. But for survival, we need more than a value system to recognize harmful and destructive behavior. We need some kind of a strategy for achieving our desired goals.

I received a letter some months ago from a lawyer in our congregation. It said in part:

> . . . What hit me hardest about a sermon I heard recently was the point that we all have an affirmative responsibility to approach our brothers and sisters who are sinning and get them back on the right track. That statement is maybe a bit overboard in that we are all sinning in one way or another and perhaps we all need to be reproved. I was thinking mainly of conduct like extramarital affairs, stealing, etc., which we may become aware of. I don't know exactly how far our responsibility goes but . . . the failure to take affirmative action to approach the person is a sin on our part and affects the whole Body of Christ, not just the persons directly involved.

This woman is wrestling with what her part is in taking a stand about the evil all around us and within us.

The Bible warns us to take evil seriously and gives us guidelines for dealing with it. In the eighteenth chapter of Genesis, God is planning judgment on the inhabitants of Sodom and Gomorrah for their personal and corporate sins. God reveals His plans, first of all, to Abraham, His friend. Often God reveals His plans to righteous people, to those who believe in Him and trust Him and we call this prophecy. The Lord says in verse 20, "Because the outcry against Sodom and Gomorrah is great. . . ." The Hebrew word translated "outcry" means "foul play" or "a cry of injustice." Terrible things are being done in those two cities and God hears the outcry and sets out to deal with this social cancer.

Abraham Strikes a Bargain

Hearing of God's plan, Abraham tries to bargain with Him. It is an astonishing dialogue. He begins by suggesting that Sodom should be spared if there are fifty righteous found there. Then he proceeds to whittle that number down to forty-five, thirty, twenty, and eventually ten. The Lord agrees. If even ten righteous citizens are found, the city will be spared.

There's a strange whimsy in this whole interchange. I find it interesting that Abraham does not intercede specifically for his nephew, Lot, who lives in Sodom. He is pleading for the whole city and all its wicked inhabitants; he is not just praying for his relatives and friends. We learn here that intercession needs to go beyond prayers for our immediate circle, our own interests and concerns.

Abraham's bargaining technique is typical of what still goes on in the Middle East today. In a bazaar, you never pay the price asked for any item. The price is just the start of bargaining.

On the occasions when I've been in the Middle East, I've

found I really enjoy this process; in fact, I sometimes get carried away by it. On one trip I was browsing in a little shop and found a lovely old brass teapot. I didn't need it, but I liked it and I asked the proprietor for the price. He said, "Twenty-four American dollars." I said, "I'll give you twelve." He said, "Twenty-two is my bottom price." I said, "I could go to fourteen." This game continued until, finally, I offered him seventeen. "No," he said, "it's eighteen." In good Middle East bazaar style, I played my trump card. I started to walk out of the shop. I thought he would probably come after me and say it was a deal and I'd win. But I had underestimated my bargaining opponent. As I was walking out the door, he yelled after me in front of all the customers, "Mister, did you travel ten thousand miles to save one dollar?" The upshot was that I now possess an $18 brass teapot.

Abraham's bargaining with the Lord is, of course, over human lives. Abraham cares about the people of Sodom. They have no idea of their impending destruction, and yet somebody who is not a Sodomite is interceding for them.

Perhaps this account of Abraham bargaining with God can be explained more theologically. In these verses Abraham is exploring God's mind. He's saying, "I know You are a just God. If there are fifty, forty, thirty, or even ten righteous people in that sin-ravaged city, aren't those worth more to You than all those sinners?" God agrees. Abraham is convinced that the key to the fate of Sodom lies not in how many are evil, but in how many are righteous. That may be a tiny minority but minorities are always the hinges on which great doors swing. It's the few who are moral and righteous (or the few who are immoral and unrighteous) who make the difference.

Entertaining Angels

As a result of this bargain, two angels go down to investigate Sodom to see if, indeed, there are ten righteous there and

Lot becomes their host. Bear in mind that Abraham has been living in a tent ever since he and Lot divided up the land. Lot, on the other hand, lives in a fine house in a big city. He seems to have prospered beyond his uncle. When the two strangers arrive, he's out there in the cool of the evening sitting near the gate as was the custom of the city elders. He leaps to his feet and invites them to come to his house. He has no idea who they are but insists that they be his guests. After an initial protest, they accept. Lot is unaware he is entertaining angels. You and I have at times that same opportunity—to entertain angels, unaware.

Just before the Civil War, a very prosperous farmer named Worthy Taylor hired a young man named Jim to do the chores for the summer. Jim milked the cows and chopped the kindling and slept in the hayloft and ate with the family. Over the course of that summer, he fell in love with Taylor's daughter and he asked for her hand in marriage. "Come now," said the farmer. "You have no money and no prospects. I'm sorry, but I can't let you marry my daughter." The summer ended and Jim packed his little carpetbag and left. Thirty-five years passed and in that time Worthy Taylor prospered. He decided to tear down his old barn and build a bigger one. In the process of doing so, he found, carved in the rafter over the hayloft where Jim had slept, Jim's full name, "James A. Garfield," by then President of the United States. He had entertained a future president—unaware.

Two friends of ours from Princeton seem to know all kinds of people in high places all over the world. I once asked them how that came about. "They weren't important when we met them," was the explanation. These friends were in the habit of taking foreign students at the university into their home to love and feed and care for them. Many of the young people became world leaders in later years. As we practice the gift of hospitality, we never know what blessings may result or which of those guests are God's special messengers.

The Reckoning

Obviously, Sodom failed the test of harboring ten righteous citizens and it was destroyed. Lot's guests were threatened with gang rape, and Genesis 19:4 says "all the people to the last man" were perpetrators of this crime. The only righteous ones, apparently, were Lot and his family.

The code of hospitality in those ancient times seems incomprehensible to us. Lot risks his own life to defend his guests and offers the mob his two virgin daughters instead. The host was responsible, at the risk of his own life or the lives of his family members, for the safety of those who were guests in his house. Lot was caught between two rotten choices, just as we are at times. Tomorrow or the next day we may have to deal with something like that, two equally abhorrent alternatives. In those times, we can only pray and ask God's help. Lot's solution, which seems so barbaric, was, in the etiquette of the day, an honorable one.

Lot makes every effort to rescue his guests from the mob and is, himself, rescued. As the crowd is about to trample Lot and break down the door of the house, the angels snatch him inside, close the door, and smite the whole crowd with blindness. Don't you love it? That's the kind of instant revenge I wish for sometimes. Sodom is then destroyed by an earthquake. We don't know exact details, but historians have concluded there was a tectonic earthquake that released either volatile sulphuric gases or petroleum or asphalt, all of which lie under the area in abundance. The earth opened, some substance ignited, and a holocaust resulted. The city's destruction is historical fact.

Only Lot, his wife, and two daughters were spared. Unfortunately, his wife was a reactionary. She couldn't help looking back. She is the spiritual kin to all those who say, "The great days of this church are in the past," or "The great days of our nation are in the past." In spite of the angels' warnings not to look back or stop anywhere, she couldn't resist doing so. She couldn't receive the good that God had for her in the future because she was so tied to what had been in the past. She is destroyed by her own reactionary spirit while Lot and his two daughters are spared.

The angels tried to rescue Lot's whole household, including his prospective sons-in-law who foolishly refused to leave. This is covenant theology. We believe that if one person in the household is a believer, the entire household is blessed. Lot warns these two young men to get out of the city. The Lord would spare their lives because they were a part of Lot's family. They decided he was jesting. If you don't take evil and its consequences seriously, you don't take God seriously. These young men are destroyed with the unrighteous not because they're evil but simply because they don't believe.

Recently, William Golding received a much deserved Nobel Prize for his works, including *Lord of the Flies. Lord of the Flies* gives the lie to the pervasive philosophy among us that people are basically good and society corrupts us. It is the story of a group of little boys whose plane crashes on a deserted island and who before long are reduced to acting like savages, perpetrators of evil on each other. The message is that a predisposition for evil is something we are born with. A human being in the natural state uses and abuses others for his or her own interests. Evil doesn't happen to us. We are the instigators of it. That conviction sets Christians apart from the secular humanists.

Provoking God's Wrath

We might do well to examine the exact nature of the evils of Sodom and Gomorrah which so incurred God's wrath. There was, of course, sexual sin. Homosexual gang rape was apparently a usual occurrence, but that is just symptomatic of the real problem. The people of Sodom were guilty of unbelief and disobedience, ignoring even the strict laws of hospitality. They didn't ask, "Who is my neighbor?" And they didn't care. Ezekiel describes the guilt of Sodom in these terms. "[Sodom] had pride, surfeit of food, and prosperous ease, but did not aid the poor and needy. They were haughty and did abominable things before me; therefore I removed them . . ." (Ezek. 16:49–50). The sin of Sodom continues in our society, in your life and mine. Our nation is subject to judgment for those same sins.

UNICEF tells us that last year forty thousand children died daily of malnutrition and infection. The Maine department of human services maintains that poverty is the ultimate cause of death annually for eleven thousand children in our own country. In five years, that figure adds up to more deaths than all the battle casualties of the Vietnam war. According to the World Health Organization, ten children die each minute in developing nations from preventable infectious diseases, but only 10 percent of the eighty million born each year in those places are immunized. In our own country, 40 percent of our poor, black urban children are not immunized. The immunization cost is less than $5.

It's sobering to realize that the sin of Sodom looks a lot like the sin of our own glorious and wonderful country. Evil is not some alien force out there somewhere. Yes, it's all-pervasive but it's personal and it's within. I bring evil to every situation. I'm devious, selfish, unloving, and judgmental. Beyond that, evil is interpersonal. When we come together, there is competition, manipulation, and exploitation. Then there is corporate evil. We perpetrate and commit evil as a church and as a nation. We are guilty of sins of commission, like the Nazis who deliberately and systematically killed millions of Jews whom they considered genetically inferior. But Sodom's sins, and ours, are also sins of omission—doing nothing about poverty and disease and hunger. We'd like to think the sins of commission are worse, that it is more evil to deliberately destroy people than to ignore them. But those subtle gradations don't seem to matter to God.

Dealing with Sin

God has provided a way to redeem the internal sin that you and I bring to every situation. The Holy Spirit can convict us and help us to repent and make restitution. We are forgiven by the grace of God in Jesus Christ. But, confession and repentance and restitution are part of that transaction. Our corporate sins as a nation or a church are another matter and we need to apply the lessons of these verses in chapter 19 to those sins. These verses indicate that there are at least three possible attitudes toward corporate sin.

First, there is indifference. That's Lot's attitude in the beginning of this story. He sits in the middle of this wicked city talking to his neighbors and enjoying the ambience. He is the embodiment of all of us who play along and say, "Who's perfect?" Tim Dearborn, our church's missions pastor, has described Lot as "a blob of jelly on roller skates." He doesn't cause any evil. He just goes with the flow and says, "Who cares?"

The second attitude is that of God Himself, who is a God of law and justice. Make no mistake about that. Because He is a God of law, He brings judgment down on Sodom. We Presbyterians take sin and God's judgment very seriously. We believe that "power corrupts and absolute power corrupts absolutely." Our system of courts at all three levels, Session, Presbytery, and General Assembly, are set up to deal with corporate and personal sin.

There is a whole movement in the church in our time to damn and blast sexual transgressors. That might seem like a godly stance, if we see Him only as a God of judgment. But the New Testament gives us a clearer picture of God in Jesus. When the disciples urge Him to bring down judgment on the Samaritans who won't receive Him, He constrains them. We see grace in operation and, sure enough, before long a good many Samaritans become believers. We must keep in mind that law and judgment are just one side of God's nature, transcended by His love and grace.

Abraham models a third attitude toward evil or sin. First of all, he avoids it geographically. He lives as far away as he can from these depraved pleasure-loving societies. David Frost once said that by means of television we invite people whom we wouldn't have as guests into our living rooms to entertain us. TV makes it more and more difficult to ignore the world's values and avoid its perverted pleasures. Abraham lived as far away as possible from the evil, but nevertheless he interceded for the evil-doers. There's an important lesson here. In the third chapter of John we read, "God so loved the world that He gave His only Son . . . for God sent the Son into the world, not to condemn the world, but that the world might be saved through Him." Abraham understands God's heart. If there's any hope for Sodom, God wants to bless and not condemn. God hears Abraham's prayer of intercession. A small righteous band is more important to Him than a great number of the unrighteous.

Sin and evil exist and God's judgment is real. Too many of us behave like those two sons-in-laws who said, "Oh, come on, you must be kidding." But God is the God of law and judgment. At the same time, grace abounds. Receive it, live it, give it, and intercede for all people as Abraham did. A bumper sticker I saw recently read, "God Bless America— and Please Hurry." That's the whimsical way of interceding for our nation. God wanted to spare Lot and his family from the destruction of Sodom but Lot was reluctant to go. The two angels were forced to grab him by the hand and drag him out of the city. He was saved almost against his will. God can do that for us if we trust Him. He can save us whether or not we're willing to be saved. If we believe that, we are counted among the righteous.

At Christmas time in 1939, with the whole world on the brink of the horrible devastation of World War II, King George VI reminded England and the world of a friend they could trust with this poem:

I said to the man at the gate of the year:
"Give me a light that I might walk safely into the unknown!"
He replied, "Go forth into the darkness, and put your hand
in the hand of God.
That shall be for you better than light, and safer than a known
way."
So I went forth, and finding the hand of God, trod gladly
into the night.
Then God led me safely toward the hills and the breaking
of day in the lone east.

11. The Final Test

Genesis 22

The story of Abraham setting out to sacrifice his beloved son, Isaac, is a shocking one. We in the Western world have an especially difficult time understanding it, perhaps because we are so inculcated with the idea of the value of every single life.

I read some interesting statistics about the resources that go into sustaining the life of the average American. We use 9,450 quarts of milk during our lifetime. Along with that, we eat 150 cows, 225 lambs, 26 sheep, 310 hogs, 26 acres of grain, and 50 acres of fruit and vegetables, not to mention all the non-edible resources we use like oil, gas, lumber, and the rest. We might wonder if we're worth it. The biblical answer is a resounding, "You bet you're worth it." God paid a price for us. We are worth the death of His own Son. Whatever it takes just to support and sustain our lives, we're worth it.

In *Crime and Punishment,* Dostoevsky wrote, "If one had to live on some high rock on such a narrow ledge that he only had room enough to stand, and the ocean and the ever-lasting darkness, everlasting tempest around him, if he had to remain standing on a square yard of space all his life, a thousand years, eternity, it were better to live so, than to die at once. Only to live, to live and live. Life, whatever it may be. Amen." This great Russian Christian understood the preciousness of life.

A Monstrous Demand

That's the mind-set most of us bring to the story we find in the twenty-second chapter of Genesis. The Lord has finally kept His promise to Abraham. Though now one hundred years old, he has a son with Sarah. We can only imagine their joy. As much as we may delight in our children, Abraham's delight was greater, for his son was his future, his inheritance, the fulfillment of his covenant with God. All of God's promises were focused on that one son. Yet we read in verses 1 and 2, "After these things God tested Abraham, and said to him, 'Abraham, here am I. Take your son, your only son Isaac, whom you love, go to the land of Moriah, and offer him there as a burnt offering.' "

What a monstrous demand. How do we explain a God who would make such a demand, and of Abraham, of all people? Abraham cut himself off from his past and his ancestors when he left Ur and Terah. He no longer has a tribe or a nation. He's been a wandering pilgrim because God had promised him a future. Now God is asking him to destroy that future. He will have nothing. God is well aware of what He is asking. Referring to Isaac, He calls him first "your son," then "your *only* son" and then "the son *whom you love.*" We are stunned that Abraham plans to obey.

The place where the sacrifice is to be made is a three-day journey away, and on the very next morning Abraham starts that journey with two young men from his household and the lad, Isaac. I'd like to write a short story or a play sometime that would cover the drama of those three days. The biblical narrative gives us no details. We've got to use our imagination. To begin with, did Abraham tell Sarah about this new development and, if so, how? "Honey, I'm going to kill our son." Did she say, "So be it," or did she say,

"Listen, you crazy old fool, the older you get the more fanatic you get. What are you saying?" If he did not tell her, then for three days he would be thinking, "When I have done this, I must go back home and face Sarah. When she asks about Isaac, how can I ever explain what I did?" Think of Abraham's dilemma.

Being misunderstood by your loved ones is sometimes the cost of discipleship. Most of us have experienced that in some degree. You may have become a Christian as a youngster or college student and your friends, or even your parents, simply didn't understand at all. They said, "You've become a fanatic." Perhaps they laughed or were scornful and you were misunderstood. Perhaps as a Christian, you've been called to some job or ministry that has none of the usual rewards of salary or prestige. Those close to you say, "Is that really what you think God wants you to do?" You are misunderstood and often by the people you really care about. That's not easy.

Jesus had the same experience. His mother and brothers tried to interrupt His ministry and bring Him back home where He would cease to be an embarrassment to them. We can imagine His mother pleading, "Come home and be a good Jewish boy. Go to the synagogue, work in the carpenter shop. Be good to your mother. Stop these attention-getting activities." Jesus was forced to tell His family that He must do God's will and not theirs.

A Father's Anguish

Abraham, friend of God, must have talked to Him often in that three-day walk. I'm sure he had many doubts along the way, just as we do. We may have thought God's message was clear but as we start off to follow His guidance, we begin to question whether or not He did, in fact, speak. Walking along with his beloved son, Abraham must have had many second thoughts. "Father, God, did You mean for me to kill this boy? That was two or three days ago and I may not have heard right. Tell me again. Tell me one more time. Maybe this whole vision came as a result of something I ate. I may have had too much wine that night. Tell me one more time and I'll be certain of Your will." All the while, God is silent. We've been there. Abraham is saying, "Lord, give me a sign," and no sign comes. He has to go on the guidance he got three days ago.

Or, what do you talk about during this journey with your beloved son, the son you waited a lifetime for? Now he's a reality and he's a beautiful lad. What do you talk about? Perhaps Abraham regaled him with the adventures he's had since he left Ur or with the exciting story of rescuing Lot from his enemies. In a day or so, Abraham will never see this boy again. It is a scenario that breaks our hearts. I'm sure it was the hardest test of Abraham's whole life—this final test.

A friend of mine tells about driving through Kentucky when he went off on a side road to see some of the more rural areas of this beautiful state. He found himself in a small town called No Hope, Kentucky. On a hunch, he drove around looking for a church and sure enough he came upon a lovely little white structure in front of which was a big sign that declared it to be "The No Hope Baptist Church." That's the church I'm sure Abraham could have joined at this point—the No Hope Baptist Church. He must have had serious misgivings. "What kind of God do I worship who would require this of me?"

When they arrive at the place of sacrifice and Abraham is making preparations, Isaac asks, "Dad, where's the lamb?" (the animal to be killed). "God will provide," answered Abraham. When he puts the wood on the altar and binds his son and lays him there, I'm sure Isaac was puzzled. "Father, what are you doing?" What did Abraham say at that point? It is only when he raises his hand to kill Isaac that the angel of God interferes. "Abraham, Abraham, do not lay your hand

on the lad." He's interrupted. We call that fresh guidance.
Just in the nick of time, God says, "I've got a new plan."

Fresh Guidance

I would suggest to you that, with all of his failings, one of
Abraham's great gifts is that he's interruptible. Since the beginning call in Ur of the Chaldees, he has been responsive
to God's voice. Thank God, he was responsive at this point
to the angel who said, "Abraham, stop." He was open to
the possibility of a new plan. He wasn't a hard-nosed fanatic
who said, "I've had my guidance from God and I'm going
to follow it whatever." He's flexible. Flexibility is a quality
lacking in a good many business leaders today, according
to Eric Bienstock. In his publication *Board Room,* he says,
"Managers' obsession with being right brings about rigidity
of thinking. That stifles creativity, discourages risk-taking, po-
larizes people over issues and leads to the recycling of old
ideas. Highly intelligent executives with large egos and top
positions to protect are usually the most effective at stifling
new ideas of others. The more intelligent the executive, the
more capable the person is of defending a position, regardless
of its merit."

We Christians, I think, tend to be guilty of this same rigidity. "God gave me the word and I'll carry it out if it kills
us all." One mark of greatness, spiritual or otherwise, is the
ability to be open to a new plan, a new idea. The church
ought to be open to the same kind of on-course correction.
What seemed like God's will a century ago or a decade ago
is not necessarily God's will now. We can do an about face
and start off in a whole new direction with no apologies
because God is still in the business of giving us fresh guidance.

Abraham is then blessed by God. His son is spared and
the covenant is reestablished. God is not playing games. He
didn't know what Abraham was going to do. That's the whole
point of free will. God has given us freedom and that means

He doesn't know what decisions we will make until we make them. After this, the final test, the angel says, "Because you have not withheld your son, God will indeed bless you." God knows that Abraham is obedient, and Abraham knows that God is trustworthy. Abraham passed the test.

The great psychiatrist Carl Jung, analyzer of human behavior and Freud's friend and colleague, came to this kind of moment of truth. He says, "Suddenly I understood that God was, for me at least, one of the most certain and immediate experiences . . . I do not believe; I know, *I know!*" Knowing surpasses believing. As a result of this final test, God *knows* about Abraham and Abraham *knows* about God.

God's Requirements

Nevertheless, we need to examine why God would make such a test. The Bible reveals to us that He's a jealous God. He cares about us. He wants us for Himself and He wants to be at the center of our lives, not on the periphery. He wants our attention. That's what worship is, focusing on God with all our heart, mind, and soul. In Philippians 3, Paul lists all of his accomplishments, all his credentials, all the things that would make him a Pharisee of the Pharisees. He says, in effect, "I count them all as garbage in order that I might gain Christ." That's Abraham's creed. His life was garbage, his son's life was of no consequence compared with knowing God. Above all else in his life, God was central.

Perhaps it should be said here that Abraham lived in a time when infant sacrifice was common practice. Perhaps that's why God gave Abraham this particular test. Abraham's neighbors, who worshiped stone idols, sacrificed their sons and daughters to their false gods. Did Abraham love the true God as much as his neighbors loved their false gods? To prove that he did, he was willing to sacrifice his son. Sociologically, we think we've progressed far beyond infant sacrifices. But have we? Suppose somebody from another

planet came to earth to examine and report back on who
we are and what we're like. What do you think that space
creature would say? "They are strange people. I think their
chief industry is war. The biggest, single item in their national
budget is for armaments. Since 3600 B.C. they have entered
into 14,531 wars, wars in which 3,640,000,000 young people
have been killed." Those are sobering figures to those of
us who are feeling smug that our civilization has progressed
far beyond the barbaric practices of Abraham's time.

Abraham passed the final test and life is full of tests. You
and I have tests all the time. The Olympics are the final tests
for athletes. We've all taken school tests and exams. At my
advanced age, I confess I still have nightmares where I am
in a classroom taking an exam for which I am totally unpre-
pared. I wake up in a cold sweat. Every day your courage
is tested, your virtue is tested, your honesty is tested. Abraham
had tests all along his pilgrimage. Some he passed and some
he failed. The final or ultimate test concerns that which is
at the center of our lives.

The Provider and the Provisions

God wants us to worship Him, He wants our love and friendship. He doesn't want to share us with anybody. He wants
to be central for Abraham and for you and me. Is God an
end in Himself or is He a means to an end? We may think
of God as somebody who has provided us with life, health,
a spouse, loving children, a rewarding career or job, a pension, and benefits. We may feel gratitude to God for all these
gifts, but that is not enough. God is asking if these things
He has given us mean more to us than He does. Isaac was
everything to Abraham—his pension, his benefits, his life,
his future, and his hope.

When God originally called Abraham saying, "Follow me,"
the risk was small, as it usually is initially for you and me.
First, he leaves home. Then he goes to Egypt and deceives

Pharaoh and God bails him out. God makes him rich. God delivers him in war. God blesses him and gives him honor. All the while, God has provided him with more and more blessings until they come to this final test in which God asks Abraham to put it all on the line. He asks this very question, "Which is first in your life—that which I have given you or Me?" God asks us that same question. Is our life centered in the Provider or the provisions? The Israelites wandered for forty years in the desert. They were faithful in spite of hard times. Once in the Promised Land, the land of milk and honey, they accumulated wealth and, somehow, it became more difficult to be faithful. Prosperity is a mixed blessing.

Like Abraham, you and I have flunked some of the tests along the way. We'll flunk others in the future. But, the test that counts is the final test. Is God more important to us than all the things we've acquired, not just material possessions, but family, friends, even our church? The final test comes in a different form for each of us. A Christian couple I know moved to a large city to begin a ministry to the very poor. They joined a commune where several families and a few singles shared a big house in what was mostly a black ghetto. For the wife, it was the most difficult thing she'd ever done. She had to share not just her husband and two babies with this extended family but, hardest of all, her beautiful wedding presents. God seemed to ask her, "Do you love your privacy and your wedding presents more than Me?"

For the husband, it was not the same kind of final test. He felt burdened by the emotional responsibility of being a husband and father and moving into a commune meant that burden would be shared. He could go off about his mission while others supplied emotional support for his wife and children. Their new move, which was the final test for the wife, was simply a welcome change for the husband.

John Wesley is one of my heroes. He was the person responsible for England's great revival. For fifty years he traveled up and down the land on horseback, preaching three or four times a day every day to miners and farmers and others who made up England's working class. But perhaps his activities were not entirely motivated by selflessness. He had an unhappy marriage. His wife was given to violence and sometimes pulled him around the house by the hair. It's possible that preaching all over England was preferable to staying at home. But whether Wesley's arduous travels were or were not a difficult test, God changed all of England through him.

A friend of mine was born into a very wealthy and powerful family. In response to God's call, Harry left the company business and became an unordained lay preacher. He held rallies all over the land and hundreds and thousands came to Jesus because of his preaching and counseling ministry. In the midst of this success, he went on a week-long retreat in the course of which God seemed to ask him, "Harry, what do you love more—Me or the ministry I've given you?" He realized the ministry meant more to him than the Lord and he has since gone back into business. The work God has given you to do can take His place as much as riches and pleasures.

In the International District in our town, my Buddhist neighbors can buy an ancestor worship kit for about $1.95. It contains two candles, four pieces of incense, all kinds of paper streamers to hang, and, best of all, a pack of fake money. It seems when Buddhists worship their ancestors, they must burn money as part of the ceremony. Thanks to the kit, you needn't burn your own money. For $1.95 you can burn pho-ney money and still honor your ancestors.

Our God demands our tithes and offerings and accepts no counterfeits, but I'm convinced He wants more than our money. He wants all of us. He wants to be the center of our attention, the One in whom we delight. The Apostle Peter flunked one of his tests. He said to Jesus, "I will never forsake You." In just a few hours, he broke that promise. A young servant girl asked, "Do you know Him?" And he replied (to put it in the vernacular) "Never saw Him before in my life." He flunked the smaller test, but that was not the final test. Later on Jesus asked, "Peter, do you love me?" With emotion, Peter swore he did. Jesus put the question a second and then a third time. That was the final test, and Peter passed.

There'll be temptations and tests for all of us this very week—perhaps even the final test. Our Creator and friend gives us comforting words through the Apostle Paul in 1 Corinthians 10:13, "No temptation has overtaken you that is not common to man. God is faithful, and he will not let you be tempted beyond your strength, but with the temptation will also provide a way of escape, that you may be able to endure it."

12. Life: Transactions and God's Actions

Genesis 23 and 24

If you're a Christian, you believe that God is in every part of life. The very hairs of your head are numbered and His hand is on you wherever you go. But suppose someone were to ask you, "Where do you see God?" What would you say? If we believe God is in our lives, we need to hunt for Him and recognize Him in those places where He is at work. God is in the numinous and in the natural. He is in the ordinary transactions of life and in the extraordinary events and circumstances of life.

A Poignant Purchase

The Genesis story continues with an ordinary transaction. Abraham is buying a burial plot. Sarah is dead and Abraham is mourning her. All of us will experience some kind of mourning during our lifetime and we'd do well to think through our ideas about mourning long before the fact.

Some time ago my wife Hazel and I were in California on business. We arrived at our motel in time to catch our favorite TV show, PBS's Masterpiece Theater series. In that night's episode of A. J. Cronin's *The Citadel*, the hero was mourning the death of his young wife who was hit by a truck. When the show ended, we started to discuss this business of mourning. What kind of mourning strikes you as appropriate? Is a loved one to be mourned a long time, a short time, forever? At what point do you move on? We had a very interesting discussion on just how we perceived we might mourn for each other—a discussion heated enough to make us glad for the separate beds that most hotels provide.

I heard about a woman who was discussing this sort of thing with her husband. "Dear, if I die first would you marry again?" He said, "Well, I've been so happy with you, I think I would." She probed further—"Would your new wife wear my fur coat?" He said, "Well, I'd hate to sell it or give it away. Yes, she probably would." "Would she drive my Mercedes?" He said, "I'd hate to sell your car. Yes, she probably would." She persisted, "Would she use my new golf clubs with the new leather bag?" "No," he said, "she's left-handed."

That's not the kind of mourning we're talking about. Abraham was genuinely mourning for Sarah and he needed a place to bury her. He was a stranger in the land of Canaan. The Hittites had allowed him, a herdsman who owned no property, to live there. To get the desired burial place, he entered into dialogue with the Hittites and his wise handling of this transaction can teach us a lot. First, testing the water, he told them that as a stranger and sojourner in their land, he realized that his presence there was contingent on their generosity. I'm sure his humility endeared him to the Hittites.

Some Shrewd Trading

But if we read between the lines, the transaction itself becomes another interesting piece of bargaining. In the vernacular, this is what happens. Abraham says, "I need a place to bury my wife." They reply that he can have anything he wants. What does he want? Abraham confesses that he has really had his eye on the Cave of Machpelah which belongs to Ephron, who happens to be sitting there among the other elders. Ephron says, "Why, of course, you can have the Cave of Machpelah and the whole plain." In this everyday transaction, two clever Middle Easterners are doing some horse trading. If Abraham wants the cave, he'll have to take the whole field. Ephron continues, "We're friends. You live here. You can have the field for nothing." Abraham protests, "I couldn't do that. I insist on paying for it." Ephron responds, very cleverly working in his price, "What's a cave and a field worth 400 shekels of silver among friends?" "I'll buy it," says Abraham. It's a wonderful dialogue.

The result of this whimsical exchange between these two sharp traders, Ephron and Abraham, is that Abraham finally owns a piece of the Promised Land. God has promised his descendants will own the whole thing some day but this field is the down payment. So, in the simple purchase of a cemetery plot, Abraham becomes the owner of a whole field and that is the first earnest money on God's promise.

God is in all our transactions, however ordinary, and we have to start looking for Him. I remember one transaction that was a wonderful lesson to me, and I'm convinced God was in it all. Some years ago, a pastor friend and I were cruising in the Caribbean, leading a seminar at sea for some clergy and their wives. The two of us were ashore in Trinidad and hurrying to get back aboard ship. As we were about to climb up the gangplank, a little man ran up. Pointing to some objects wrapped in a handkerchief, he said, "I've got two fine watches here, an Accutron and an Omega. You can have them for $25 apiece." With that, he let us peek at them. My friend mentioned that between us we had just $20. "Sold!" said our salesman. We boarded the ship with our new-found treasures to find the Accutron was actually an "Acatron" and the Omega was an "Omica." They weren't worth even $3 each. The Lord seemed to say to me, "Larson, there is larceny in your heart." As W. C. Fields used to say, "You can't cheat an honest man." I'd like to think that since then I have been much less judgmental of those caught with a hand in the cookie jar.

A Romantic Errand

We move on now to Genesis 24 where we read about God's action in the numinous, the mysterious. This love story in four acts begins with Abraham sending his steward on an errand. Perhaps the steward was the same Eliezer we read about in Genesis 15:2, who was to have inherited Abraham's goods and property, had Ishmael not been born. In this transaction, conditions are laid down. Abraham is determined that Isaac, now grown, should not marry a local girl, a Canaanite. The steward is to journey to Abraham's homeland and find a young woman among his kinsmen. Isaac is not to go along. The young woman must be willing to return with the steward.

You might wonder about this old father who sits back and leaves this important task to someone else. A friend of mine with a Coast Guard commission tells of being on a ship captained by a friend of his. On one occasion, my friend went into the captain's quarters to find that gentleman wearing a kilt and playing a bagpipe. My friend asked, "Does your crew know how much fun you have as captain of this ship?" "Don't you realize," was the answer, "that the captain is the only guest on board? Everybody else works." Apparently, it was not too unlike that in an ancient tribal society. The chief doesn't do anything. He gives orders. Eliezer is given these important errands and told that "God will send His angel before you." Eliezer believes that God will not fail him, and he sets out. Later on, in verse 27, we find him praying in thanksgiving, "As for me, the Lord has led me in the way to the house of my master's kinsmen."

This might be a good place to bring up the old question of whether or not there is only one right person for each of us. If you think I plan to answer that, you're mistaken. For one thing, I don't know. Are so-called "love marriages" far happier than the arranged ones of Abraham's time, a system still practiced in a good part of the world? We have several Oriental couples in our church whose marriages were planned by their parents. One man never even met his wife-to-be until she got off the plane from Korea, and these two seem blissfully happy. We have to conclude that sometimes our elders know what we need better than we do ourselves, but I couldn't sell that idea to my three children.

Act two features Eliezer and Rebekah. When Eliezer gets to Mesopotamia and the city of his master's birth, he asks the Lord for a sign. The girl he is to choose will respond in a certain way when he speaks to her. Eliezer expected God to guide him and set up precise conditions for recognizing God's guidance when it came. He was a listener, and that's a valuable asset.

There's a story I love about Thomas Edison. It seems he was asked to sell Western Union his original telegraph ticker for their museum. How much did he want for it? He told them he'd have to think about it and went home to discuss the matter with his wife. Her advice was that he should ask "not a penny less than $20,000." He was dumbfounded. "Twenty thousand dollars for this old piece of hardware?" At the meeting with the Western Union representatives he was again asked his price. He felt too embarrassed to name the exorbitant figure his wife had suggested. For about thirty seconds, he said nothing, at which point one of the executives jumped in. "How about $150,000?" Edison claimed that experience taught him that he talked too much. It's a story to make listeners out of all of us.

Most of all, we can profit when we listen to God, our ultimate friend who wants the best for us. Eliezer did that.

After meeting this extraordinary woman at the town well, Eliezer accompanies her to her brother Laban's house. He witnesses to Laban, telling him how God has answered his prayers and that his sister has met all his requirements. Surely she was meant to be Isaac's wife. Laban believes this stranger, but he urges Rebekah to wait ten days before leaving. This brave young woman, however, agrees to go back at once. She sets out with a stranger to a strange land to marry a man she's never seen because she believes it is God's will for her.

The concluding scene, starring Isaac and Rebekah, is the happy ending of our love story. Isaac is out in the field in the evening meditating when he sees the caravan coming. The last verse of the chapter tells it all. "Then Isaac brought her into the tent, and took Rebekah, and she became his wife; and he loved her. So Isaac was comforted after his mother's death." It's so beautiful and so simple. Isaac, who was grieving for his mother, takes the new wife God has given him to his bosom and is comforted. I love it.

Finding God's Guidance

It seems to me we can draw some simple conclusions from this love story. First of all, God does guide very specifically—sometimes. I don't play golf, but something Jack Nicklaus says about how he plays the game gives us insight into this incident. "I never hit a shot, not even in practice, without having a sharp, in-focus picture of it in my head. It's like a color movie. First, I see the ball where I want it to finish. Then, the scene quickly changes and I see the ball going there—its path, trajectory, and shape, even its behavior on landing. Then, the next scene shows me making the kind of swing that will turn the previous images into reality." We can't argue with Jack Nicklaus. That system has certainly worked for him. Eliezer did something like this. He envisioned ahead how God might guide him. He set down specific conditions and God honored them. That can work for you and me. Picture good things happening to you. Imagine them and claim them and see if God won't honor that.

Second, the sign Eliezer asked for was a specific one but nothing spectacular. The right girl at the well would not just draw water for him, but would, in addition, offer to draw water for his ten camels. He was looking for a young lady who was compassionate enough to go the second mile. Imagine the time and effort involved in drawing water for ten camels. By this small test, the steward found Rebekah was generous and that she understood and loved animals—

wonderful attributes for the wife of a nomadic herdsman. The qualifications Eliezer was looking for were essential for the mate of his master.

In verse 16, we find that she was beautiful. That was a bonus, not one of his requirements. The Bible, being the earthy chronicle it is, records that additional bonus. "The maiden was very fair." I suspect that those of you who are unmarried have some conditions too. I did. I prayed for years and said, "Lord, first of all, she's got to love You with her whole heart. Then she has to be beautiful. And third, she has to be intelligent." I got all three of those but, unlike Eliezer, I didn't ask that she be generous, or kind, or helpful. Those qualities were a bonus. Eliezer's requirements were on target. He knew exactly the kind of person Isaac needed, a kinswoman who was kind and generous and who cared about animals.

We have been talking about trusting God to guide us in the ordinary and extraordinary transactions of life. In those that we've examined, with whom do you identify? Perhaps you feel like Abraham, who is old and needed the help of God and someone else to fulfill his destiny. Unable to go himself, he was forced to trust God and his servant with this important task. You may have been in Eliezer's situation on more than one occasion. Someone has given you a mission impossible. You feel you can't do it. Eliezer believed that God would go before him, and that's a good word for you. Do you identify with Rebekah? She, of course, is the real heroine of this story. She walks unflinchingly into the unknown. She believes this is God's will for her and she bets her life on it. With affecting heroism, she starts on a perilous journey with an unknown man to an unknown land and an unknown husband.

Isaac has a much more passive role in this story and you may identify with him. He trusts God to give him the right spouse. He sees Rebekah and takes her to himself and loves her just as she is. Nobody's perfect and even Rebekah must have some faults. Isaac could have been like some of us who are no sooner married to the person of our choice than we start criticizing or trying to change our beloved. Isaac could have said, "She's too thin. I like plump girls." Or, "I like blue eyes. Hers are brown." Or, "Her nose is too big or too small." Instead, he accepted the whole package as a gift from the Lord and loved her all the days of his life.

We can learn from Isaac. Those of us who are married need to let our spouses know how lucky we feel to have them. That's all part of trusting God. We can't say those affirmative things often enough. "Honey, am I lucky you waited for me." Or, "Am I lucky you are still with me, after all these years. Thank you."

The play "Our Town," by Thornton Wilder, is a story about the magic of the ordinary. In the course of the play the heroine, Emily, dies and returns as the unseen visitor in her old home. She tries desperately to communicate with her family how much they need to savor each precious ordinary moment of life. We all need to do that and to see God's hand in even the smallest pleasure—a cup of hot coffee in the morning, a hot shower, clean clothes, sunshine, work to do. We find God in all those ordinary transactions of everyday life but He is also in the numinous, in the extraordinary. Expect Him to be your friend in both and in every part of the journey of your life.

13. Messages from Home

Genesis 25

Identity is perhaps one of the great central themes of the Bible. In both Old and New Testaments, God's word tells us who we are. "You are a chosen people." "Before you were born I thought of you. I formed you." "You who were dead are now alive." "You are forgiven." "You are a priest." "You are light, you are salt, you are leaven." "You are no longer strangers, sojourners, but fellow citizens with the saints, members of the household of God." The Bible over and over again gives us clear messages about who God's people are. We are those whom He has called to be His friends.

I was told about an interesting tombstone in northern Wisconsin. Under the deceased's name and the date of his birth, is this epitaph. "In 1962 he bowled 300." The great achievement of that man's life was that he once bowled a perfect game. It would appear that he wanted most of all to be remembered for this modest claim to fame.

Getting the Right Message

We all have the power to make choices about who we are in spite of society's attempt to put us in a mold. We are bombarded with messages on all sides from groups and individuals, from organizations and institutions, messages telling us who we are. The other day a lady was making her first deposit at a local bank. The manager came out to welcome this new account and reassure her, "Madam, in this bank you are not just a number, you are two digits, a dash, a letter of the alphabet, another dash and two more digits."

Sometimes life's messages are subtle. Last year I read a column in our local paper about a beer distributor who for over a year now has been giving free beer to a local nursing home once a week. Every Thursday night they have a beer party, and, surprisingly enough, over this one-year period no deaths have occurred in the home on Wednesday. These senior citizens have gotten the message. Someone cares enough to throw a party for them every Thursday night.

Messages come in all sizes and shapes and are often funny. Outside of the cafeteria at the University of Colorado, a sign says, "Shoes Required to Eat in the Cafeteria." You guessed it. Under that some wit had penned with a magic marker, "Socks May Eat Wherever They Wish."

All kinds of messages come to each of us, messages both positive and negative that shape our lives and affect our destiny. A friend of mine is a pastor in Connecticut and a member of his congregation, Dr. Bernard Siegl, is a surgeon at the Yale New Haven Hospital. On one occasion during surgery, his patient suddenly stopped breathing. All life signs ceased. The surgeon, at that point, turned to this apparently dead man and said, "Henry, I don't think your time has come yet." Within seconds, all the vital signs started up again. The anesthesiologist who witnessed all of this said simply, "I don't believe it." The patient had responded to a non-medical message from his doctor.

Sir William Osler, the dean of North American medicine and a great Christian man, said once that the chances of surviving tuberculosis depend more on what is in the patient's head than what is in his chest. Messages we receive from the world around us determine, to a large degree, our illness or wellness.

I remember talking to a black pastor of an amazing church located in the poorest area of Chicago, where most congregations are struggling to survive. His church is jammed for two or three services every Sunday. I asked him to explain his success. He said, "It's very simple, I just tell people who they are." You and I have the authority to tell people who they are and who they can be if they have claimed the friendship God offers in Jesus Christ.

Twins with a Destiny

Let's see what the Bible has to say about this matter of our identity and our feelings of worth. The Bible is the ultimate source of psychology and life because it's a sort of owner's manual. God made us. His word tells us what we are and what we can be. In our story in Genesis 25, Rebekah is about to give birth. She and Isaac have been waiting and praying for a child as Isaac's father waited and prayed for him for so long. Children who are wanted for a long time are, it seems to me, especially blessed. Joseph was the long awaited first-born of his mother, Rachel. Samuel, the prophet, was the result of the agonized prayers of his previously barren mother, Hannah. Children who have been prayed for and waited for and wanted so desperately can't help receiving positive messages.

Rebekah feels strange movements in the womb during her pregnancy and she goes to a place of prayer and asks God what it all means. The Lord tells her there are twins in the womb. Each of these two will father a nation. Then she is told that, "The elder will serve the younger." The usual law of primogeniture will not prevail here.

Twins are delivered, and the first one comes forth all red and hairy and they call him "Hairy," which is what Esau means in Arabic. The second little guy while still in the womb seems to understand his position. The second-born gets nothing. For the blessing and inheritance, he must come out first.

Symbolically, he is born with his hands on his brother's heels. Seeing this drama, the parents name this second son Jacob, meaning "Supplanter" in Hebrew. Now I'm sure they loved this boy and considered this kind of a cute name. The first-born was given a legitimate name, Hairy, and the second got one indicating he was tricky and conniving. These loving parents were already sending messages to their sons.

These two boys grew up and in describing them, the text uses these stark and powerful words that somehow tell the whole tragic drama. "When the boys grew up, Esau was a skillful hunter, a man of the field, while Jacob was a quiet man, dwelling in tents. Isaac loved Esau, because he ate of his game; but Rebekah loved Jacob." Esau was his dad's favorite. Jacob was the favorite of his mother, but that was of no consequence in that patriarchal society. The birthright came solely through the father. He is the one with the power and blessing to confer. I'm sure Isaac was fond of Jacob, but it was Esau who could make his eyes light up. He delighted in him. The hunter had his father's approval as over against his quiet brother. This is the kind of real life drama that still goes on in families. If there is more than one child, one seems to have the special blessing of one or both parents. It's not simply a matter of who the parents love the most. One has the power to make their hearts sing just by coming into the room. He/she "can do no wrong."

The Crucial Messages

There's no doubt that, next to God's own messages, the most influential messages we receive are messages from home. Families can be God's best instrument in finding our identity, or they can be the biggest stumbling block to understanding who we really are. Every psychological school agrees that the family is perhaps the most important single influence in most of our lives. Freud took that idea even farther. He claimed that prenatal and postnatal messages continue to be determining factors in our psychic well-being, even into our adult years. Psychoanalysis attempts to help us understand those early messages, work through the destructive ones, and find new ones.

Much more recently, transactional analysis has been telling us that long after our parents or the authority figures in our lives have died, the tapes of their admonitions continue to play inside us and shape us for better or for worse. Salvadore Menuchin, the father of something called family therapy, claims nobody gets sick alone. Your family has conspired to bring about your emotional illness and to keep you ill. In treating patients, he insists that the whole family come for therapy and decide together to work toward the patient's recovery.

When Mother Teresa received her Nobel Prize she was asked, "What can we do to help promote world peace?" "Go home and love your family" was her answer. That seems too simple, but perhaps it's not. So many of the world's disturbed people—the hijackers, assassins, rapists, child molesters—turn out to be the products of very unhealthy and unhappy homes. Perhaps we could take a giant step toward changing the world by loving the people who are presently in our care, for whom we have responsibility.

Recently, Hazel and I and another couple about our age had the privilege of meeting with some younger couples, most of whom had been married about ten years. We four veterans were supposed to tell them how we had managed to stay married so long and give some advice on creating a positive family life. Being four different people, we had four different kinds of answers. But we all agreed on one thing— the importance of saying, doing, and being love to the other. Your family members need to know how valuable and important they are. Give them a word of grace. You can't tell your children often enough, "You are special." "You are worthwhile." "You are loved."

What did your family say about you? What are they still

telling you? I hope they told you that you are a gift of great worth, that you are a joy and a delight. That's true. Or, perhaps you felt unwanted, of no worth, a nuisance, demeaned, misunderstood.

Dr. Sammy Coopersmith, a professor of psychology at the University of California, has completed a research project on self-esteem in boys and men. I'm sure his results would apply to women too. He says, first of all, "We found no consistent relation between self-esteem and physical attractiveness, height, the size of the boys' family, early trauma, breast or bottle feeding in infancy or the mother's principal occupations—i.e., whether she worked or whether she was home all the time. Even more surprising, our subject—self-esteem—depended only weakly, if at all, on family social position or income level."

Here's what the study reveals about the boys with high self-esteem: "We were struck first and foremost by the close relationships that existed between these boys and their parents. The parents' love was not necessarily expressed by extreme shows of affection, or the amounts of time they spent with their children. It was manifested by interest in the boys' welfare, concern about their companions, availability for discussion of the boys' problems and participation in congenial, joint activities. The mother knew all, or most of her son's friends. The father and mother gave many other signs that they regarded him as a significant person who was inherently worthy of their deep interest. Basking in this appraisal, the boy came to regard himself in a similar, favorable light."

Family messages about your worth are not always explicit. I remember my mother being horrified about some family friends who did not share her reverence for new clothes. "Do you know what they do?" she would ask. "The moment they get anything new they put it on immediately and wear it until it's worn out." (That always made sense to me.) In our family, we saved new clothes for Sunday. After a couple of years, in which time they were, in my case, mostly outgrown, they were ratty enough for everyday wear. It was a practice that said a lot about our family's feelings of worth.

A friend of mine tells a similar story about his boyhood. Every morning the milkman delivered a bottle of fresh cream to be used for their cereal. But somehow they never finished the cream from the previous day and his mother insisted they do so before they could start the new. That meant that the cream was always one day old and sometimes beginning to sour. If she had just thrown the old cream away one of those mornings, they would have enjoyed fresh cream from then on. Apparently that was unthinkable.

A pastor I know tells a heart-breaking story from his childhood. He was his mother's first child and she died twelve days after his birth. His father married again and had several more children. His stepmother was very kind to him but he could never please his father. Every Washington's Birthday, the family would plant peas. If he planted the rows straight, he was too slow. If he was fast enough, the rows were crooked. He heard nothing but criticism from his dad. Later on during his college years he wanted to spend a summer at a logging camp. When his father refused to let him go, my friend rebelled and announced he was going anyway. With tears in his eyes, the father said, "Son, you broke my heart once when you caused your mother's death. I can't let that happen again." The reason for all those negative messages over the years was suddenly clear. For the sake of his own well-being, my friend has long since forgiven his father.

An Expedient Trade

The rivalry between the twins born to Isaac and Rebekah comes to a dramatic crises in the well-known story of the selling of the birthright. Esau returns home from an unsuccessful day of hunting and he is hungry—in fact, famished. His brother, the quiet man, is making a pot of stew and he asks for some. Jacob has a condition. "If you'll sell me your birthright." "I'm about to die," says Esau. "Of what use is a birthright to me?" He consents and makes the trade for a pot of lentils and some bread. He has traded a future blessing to nourish a present existence.

In later chapters we read how, with the help of Rebekah, Jacob cheats his father and again steals the birthright from his brother. Hated by his brother and his father, Jacob is eventually forced to flee for his life, but his chicanery has gotten him the birthright. Can such a despicable man actually be the one to inherit God's promises to Abraham?

The Bible, friends, deals in realism—life as it is. Certainly Esau was a good ol' boy. If I had to pick between Jacob and Esau for six weeks of backpacking in the mountains, I'd pick Esau every time. He was an athletic outdoorsman. He was uncomplicated. We find later that he was a forgiving man. In confrontation with his brother, he did not kill him, but instead forgave him. He was a man of honor and good intentions, and I'm sure, full of charm. Perhaps his charm was his fatal flaw. He lived for the moment. He wanted instant gratification. He had no long-range plans. He unwisely bargained to gain something of no lasting value.

Pursuing the Right Stuff

Jacob, on the other hand, connived and cheated for the ultimate prize. In the long run, the parental blessing was inconsequential. The first-born son with the honorable name and blessing from his father ends up as a man of little consequence. The conniver and the cheat understands what is valuable and worthy of pursuit. He uses every power at his disposal to obtain the spiritual blessing. Jacob wanted the right stuff. He had long-range, spiritual goals. He was even willing to cheat to get God's blessing. Ultimately, God chose him, but not because He rewards cheats. Rather, the message seems to be that the single-minded pursuit of God and His blessings is even more important than ethical conduct. Do the things we are pursuing in life have eternal worth? That's the real test for all of us. Jacob passed the test and Esau, that charming, forgiving, honorable man, failed.

Malcolm Muggeridge, the English Christian, speaks to this issue as he talks about his own pursuit of that which is of lasting value. "I may, I suppose, regard myself as being a relatively successful man. People occasionally stare at me in the street. That's fame. I can fairly easily earn enough to qualify for admission to the highest slopes of Inland Revenue [the British IRS]. That's success. Furnished with money and a little fame, even the elderly, if they care to, can partake of trendy diversions. That's pleasure. It might happen once in a while that something I said or wrote was sufficiently heeded to persuade myself that it represented a serious impact on our times. That's fulfillment. Yet I say to you, and I beg of you to believe me, multiply these tiny triumphs by a million, add them all together and they are nothing, less than nothing, a positive impediment, measured against one draught of that Living Water that Christ offers to the spiritually thirsty."

If you receive destructive or unhappy messages from home, forget them. If you are given positive messages, rejoice. In the case of Jacob and Esau, the guy who received the bad messages prevailed over the guy who got the good ones. Like Jacob, keep your eye fixed on that highest of all prizes. "Seek ye first the Kingdom of God and all these things shall be added unto you."

14. Detours in the Life of Faith

Genesis 27–31

The story told in chapters 27 through 31 of Genesis sounds like a soap opera—a sort of Jewish "Dynasty." If we could get the right actors and stage it on noontime TV, we could attract an audience of millions. In chapter 27, we continue the story of Jacob, one of the twins born to Isaac and Rebekah. He and his mother betray his father and his older brother, Esau. It's a sordid tale. First of all, the old father, who is blind and dying, says to his beloved Esau, the hunter, the macho man, "Before I die, go out in the field, and hunt some game (perhaps venison) for me and prepare me the kind of savory stew I like so well. After I eat it, I will bless you." The faithful Esau goes immediately.

The Stolen Blessing

Rebekah, having heard this exchange, conspires to deceive her husband and get the blessing for Jacob. She sends him to get a couple of goats and she makes an ersatz venison stew. In the meantime, she dresses Jacob in Esau's clothes and covers his hands with animal skins so that the blind Isaac will mistake him for his brother and give him the blessing. When Jacob enters with the stew, the old man seems a little suspicious for he asks, "Are you really Esau?" and asks to feel him. He eats the stew and can't seem to tell that it's not his favorite venison stew. He wants to know how he got the game so quickly, and Jacob blasphemes. He says, "Because the Lord your God granted me success." He lies before God and his father, using God's name. Nevertheless, his masquerade works and his father blesses him.

When the older son returns, the hoax is discovered. Esau cries out in anguish, "Have you but one blessing, my father? Bless me, even me also." But his father explains sorrowfully that there is but one blessing and his brother has it.

We parents identify with Isaac. When our children have broken lives and broken dreams as a result of something we have done inadvertently or otherwise, we'd like to fix it all up, but we can't. Isaac cannot make things right for Esau. He can't give him the blessing that was stolen. He has to give him a secondhand blessing, and this breaks Isaac's heart.

Esau is so angry he plots to kill Jacob. Rebekah, who has been the instrument of all this mischief, realizes that this situation may result in the loss of both of her sons. Jacob will be killed and his murderer will be forced to flee for his life. To undo the mischief she has set afoot, she manages to get Isaac to send Jacob back to Mesopotamia to find a wife for himself from among her kinsmen.

It's interesting to speculate on Rebekah's motives throughout this narrative. Is she trying to cooperate with God who told her before the boys were born that the elder would serve the younger? Are her actions designed to make sure the prophecy will come to pass? Does she doubt that God will bring this about in His own way and in His own time? She may have been trying to manipulate God to make sure He would keep His word, especially since Jacob was her favorite. If Rebekah and Jacob had not deceived Isaac, the blessing would have gone, as it must, to the elder, and that was obviously not God's plan. It seems to me that in many situations we have this same choice that Jacob and Rebekah had. We can trust in the sovereignty of God or we can be looking for ways to help Him out. That's an important lesson of the drama we read here.

Dreams and Promises

Jacob, fleeing for his life, arrives at Bethel and makes camp. All the scheming and striving are over and he has won his prize. During the night, God initiates an encounter. All true worship is initiated by God. We don't come to church saying, "Please, please be among us." We come believing that God is waiting for us and looking for us. God appears in a dream or a vision and we have come to understand that dreams and visions are often more important than reality. Einstein once said that imagination is more powerful than knowledge, and those things Einstein imagined have changed the world as we know it for all time. Our capacity for dreaming, for allowing God to be part of those dreams, will affect our present and our future.

Reality for Jacob was a life of guilt and fear and loneliness. In that state, God didn't have a chance to deal with him. Instead He chose a time when Jacob was asleep and defenseless to sneak up on him with a dream. I've had that experience, and I'm sure you have. God interrupts our sleep and gives us an insight, a word of hope, or a vision. Jacob's dream concerns a ladder, in fact, the same ladder that inspired the old song many of us learned as kids, "We Are Climbing Jacob's Ladder." As described in the Scripture, the ladder seems more like a ramp, a gateway to Heaven on which God's messengers are continually moving up and down.

But, most important in this vision at Bethel, God gives Jacob much the same promise that He made to his father and his grandfather. At the end of the promise (Genesis 28:15) we find a wonderful text that we would do well to put on our desk, dashboard, locker, refrigerator door, or anyplace where we would see it constantly: "Behold, I am with you and will keep you wherever you go. . . ." The promise that God gave Jacob here is the same promise He gives to us. First of all, He promises His presence—"I'll be with you." Emmanuel—God with us, with Abraham, Isaac, Jacob, with you and with me. Second, God promises His protection—"I will keep you wherever you go." Third, God promises His prevenience—"I will bring you back to this land. I will not leave you until I have done that which I have spoken."

In Romans 8:28, we read that "in everything, God works for good with those who love Him, who are called according to His purpose." In all of Jacob's shameful behavior toward his brother and his father, God is working out His purpose.

Bargaining with God

Jacob experiences this time of genuine worship, a firsthand encounter with God, and before he moves on he prays. It's a bargaining prayer, but bear in mind that, as far as we know, this is his first prayer. The bargain is that he will build a place of worship on that very spot and give a tithe to the Lord, if, in return, God will take care of his needs and give him food and clothing and enable him to return in peace to his father's house. Before this time, he is heir to the promise that God gave to Abraham and Isaac. Now his relationship is a personal one. God has dealt with him directly and is no longer just the God of his ancestors. In this encounter God is saying, "I am *your* God, Jacob."

Do you remember the time when you prayed your own first prayer and established that kind of personal relationship with God? It might have been on a high school or college retreat. For the first time, perhaps around a campfire, you were aware that God existed and cared about you. You may have prayed one of those bargaining prayers. "Oh, Lord, if I can get a date with Mary on Friday night, I'll give You my life." Or, "God, if I could pass Algebra III, I'll give You my life." Our first prayers are often attempts to make a deal with God and God doesn't seem to mind. That's the kind of prayer Jacob makes after this dramatic encounter.

I met a pastor at a conference in Indiana a number of years ago, and I asked him how he happened to be called to the ministry. He said, "It's an embarrassing story. I was on the boxing team in college and for three years I had never won a bout. There was a big match at the beginning of my senior year and I prayed, "Lord, if I can win this match I'll give You my life. Well, I knocked the guy out in the first round."

A Bride Too Many

Jacob continues on to Haran and meets Rachel at the well. As with his parents, it was love at first sight. He asks his Uncle Laban for her hand in marriage and is told that the price is seven years of service. The seven years finally pass and the wedding night arrives. I'm sure Jacob felt it was all worthwhile as he crawled into the wedding tent. However, in the morning, he wakes to find his bride is Rachel's older sister, Leah, the one with the weak eyes. We might wonder if Jacob didn't have a similar eye problem, if he had not noticed before this that the woman was not his beloved Rachel. Laban justifies his trickery on the grounds that he could not marry off the younger sister while the older one was unmarried. He says Jacob can have Rachel as well, if he works seven more years. Jacob ends up serving Laban for fourteen years and in return he gets two wives. Tricky Jacob seems to have met his match in Laban.

In chapter 30, the two wives begin to fight over Jacob. Leah, who was never Jacob's choice, bears three sons, each time hoping this will gain her husband's love and favor. Rachel, so far barren, arranges for Jacob to sire two sons by her maid. Leah, not to be outdone, offers Jacob her maid, and two more sons are born. (This is all in the Bible. I didn't make it up.)

This furious competition comes to its climax in the story of the mandrakes. Leah's son Reuben has found two in the field and presents them to his mother. Mandrakes were considered an aphrodisiac and Rachel, thinking they will be of use in her attempt to conceive, asks for some. To get Leah to agree, Rachel promises she will give Jacob to her for the night. Poor Jacob is a pawn between these two women, a helpless victim of their trading and bartering. The rivalry continues and the upshot of it all is that the two wives and their two maids have between them twelve sons—the patriarchs of the twelve tribes of Israel. So, even in this strange tale, we see God's purposes being carried out.

With the birth of Joseph, Rachel's first son, Jacob decides to leave and return to his homeland. Laban agrees to pay him his wages by giving him certain goats and lambs. Jacob, like his mother before him, doesn't believe God will bring him the success He has promised and he has a plan to help Him out. Since all the speckled and spotted goats and all the black lambs are to be his, Jacob figures out a way to do some selective breeding to produce only speckled or striped goats and only black lambs. Meantime, over the next six years, Laban continues to try to outwit Jacob and changes his rate of pay ten different times.

A Peace Treaty

Finally, while Laban is shearing his sheep, Jacob starts back home with his two wives and their two maids and his twelve children all on camels and with all his acquired livestock. In leaving, Rachel has stolen her father's household gods, clay figures. Laban pursues them, intending to punish them and perhaps even kill them. However, enroute, God appears to Laban and tells him to "say not a word to Jacob, either good or bad."

When these two shady characters, each suspicious of the other, are once again face to face, they declare a truce and make a covenant with each other. They build a pillar of stone and call it Mizpah, meaning "watch point," and promise not to pass over the heap to harm each other. This is the origin of the famous Mizpah benediction that many Christian people say as they conclude a meeting. "The Lord watch between me and thee while we are absent one from the other." Fortunately, the relationship between Jacob and his father-in-law ended in a covenant rather than in anger and bloodshed. Someone has said, "It's wise not to argue with a fool because somebody may come along and not know which is which."

Two recent covers of *Time* magazine provided a wonderful parable. One cover depicted the two men of the year back to back, Ronald Reagan and Yuri Andropov, the now deceased Russian chairman. The message seemed obvious that the nations of the world were holding their breath while these two super leaders continued to operate back to back, with no attempts at reconciliation. An earlier cover of the same publication showed the Pope moving to embrace the man who had tried to assassinate him. The Mizpah benediction is a reminder that we are to make peace with our enemy and be reconciled.

God's Plans and Purposes

These five chapters of Genesis, 27 through 31, interweave two great themes—the politics of life and the sovereignty of God. It's sometimes hard to believe that God is sovereign as we see all the tricky dealings of life in the church and in business and even in the family. It's difficult to see God's hand in all those weird goings-on. We tend to see God only in the Holy. We see Him as Jacob did, at Bethel with the angels ascending and descending to do His will. It's not as easy to see Him in all the trickery and deceit, all the things that seem to be detours in His plan and purpose.

The basic issue is: are we using God or is He using us? If you've given God your life, He is sovereign in it, and I believe that everything that happens to you will eventually serve His ends. In Jacob's case, God used even the treachery, the deceit, and the betrayal to work out His purpose. For example, Jacob would never, of his own accord, have married Leah. He didn't love her and didn't want her. He was tricked into taking her as his wife. If there had been no Leah, there would have been no Moses, for he was of the house of Levi, Leah's third son. There would have been no twelve tribes to make up the Israelite nation. God used Laban's trickery to make Leah a part of His plan. God can be in the tawdry, the everyday, the politics of life that we all engage in.

I recently read a letter from a lawyer in Australia. He had just been to Kenya and he had written about what perhaps is one of the worst slums in the world on the outskirts of Nairobi.

At about 4:00 P.M. I walked through the slums. . . . I picked my way through the maze of deprivation to a hut where three brothers lived their lives. I knocked on the door and entered. My apprehension vanished in a moment as about a dozen children emerged in the half light and started leaping up in the air. They were all over me in a moment of spontaneous childishness. I, too, jumped up and down with shouting kids clinging to my arms and legs and whatever else they could grab. It was a welcome like none I have known before and am never likely to know again. . . . We engaged in a sing-song amongst twenty or so raucous kids. . . .

It was a delightful experience but nothing compared with what was to come. Then came the moment which to my dying day I will never forget. From the side of the room came a quiet, clear voice: "We pray for the people of Australia, for Ned and his family," and from the group came an equally clear and quiet response, "Jesus, remember them when You come into Your Kingdom." In the middle of Africa, a group of slum kids in a reverence and earnestness previously unexperienced by me, were holding up before God the people of Australia. I thought of Australia stupefied in the euphoria of the America's Cup victory and completely oblivious of the existence of the Matari Valley slums. The incongruity of it all came down on me like a ton of bricks and I thought to myself, "God, if Australia has any hope at all, it will be because of kids like this."

In the politics of life it seems unnatural that these poor slum dwellers would have a concern for the people of privilege in Australia.

One of the lessons of Jacob's story is that we need not take our own performance too seriously. We are both betrayer and betrayed in all sorts of situations. Life is like that. We are all Rebekah; we're all Jacob; we are all Laban; we're all Rachel; we're all Leah. Our lives don't proceed in an orderly, circumscribed fashion. We all seem to experience many detours in the life of faith. But perhaps from a God's-eye view they are not detours at all.

In reality, there are no detours in the life of faith. God, our friend and advocate, is working His will in the politics of life. He is present in the Holy. May we echo the Apostle Paul who wrote in the eighth chapter of his letter to the Romans, "For I am sure that neither death, nor life, nor angels, nor principalities, nor things present, nor things to come, nor powers, nor height, nor depth, nor anything else in all creation, will be able to separate us from the love of God in Christ Jesus our Lord."

15. Demand Your Blessings

Genesis 32 and 33

The Bible tells us, "It is a fearful thing to fall into the hands of the living God" (Heb. 10:31). That being the case, our private or corporate worship ought never to be dull. Being in the presence of the living God, alone or in company with a family of believers, is fearful. Chapters 32 and 33 of Genesis give us an account of Jacob falling into the hands of the living God. The story makes it especially clear what it is He has in mind for us, for all people.

Though Jacob comes into the presence of the living God through some unique circumstances, some aspects of his situation are universal. First of all, a lot of us come into God's presence in a special way when we are desperate, when we have bottomed out. That's the case for Jacob. His mother is dead and he is returning home after a twenty-year absence. In this moment of truth, he has to face the brother he has cheated out of both the blessing and the birthright. Jacob, who has by now become a wealthy man with two wives, two concubines, eleven sons, one daughter, and all kinds of flocks and herds, panics when he learns that Esau is coming out to meet him with four hundred men.

As usual, however, Jacob comes up with a plan to save himself. He divides his family and the flocks and herds into two groups, on the assumption that his brother will come upon one of the groups and the other will be spared. If Jacob is lucky, he will be in the latter half. Next, he sends ahead all kinds of gifts that are intended to soften his brother up. He sends on wave after wave of livestock, over 550 animals in all, and each time the servant is instructed to inform Esau that these presents are from his brother Jacob. It's not a bad strategy. We have said that two of the recurring themes of the biblical narrative are faith and unbelief and, for Jacob, this is a time of unbelief. He has stopped trusting the Lord and is doing everything in his power to save himself.

Having taken all these measures, Jacob prays an interesting prayer. He reminds God that twenty years ago he came across the Jordan fleeing for his life with nothing but a staff. Now, thanks to God's blessing, he has two whole companies of wives, children, servants, flocks, and herds. Since God did all of this for him, He must surely want to continue to bless him. Jacob is in deep trouble with his brother, and he pleads with God to continue to help.

For Jacob, alone and faced with the defeats of the past and the choices for the future, this is an existential moment. God uses the circumstances of life to help us turn to Him. Our destructive behavior has a way of catching up to us and the moment of reckoning comes as it did for Jacob. We cheat in a marriage, certain our spouse will never know, and one day that moment of reckoning arrives. Or, we fill out our tax return, omitting just a few little items of our income, and one day we get notice of an impending audit. All those shortcuts to success, like cheating on a school exam, or cutting corners in business, have a way of ultimately crashing in on us. We tell ourselves lies. We say we can get off drugs or booze anytime we want to, and one day all the self-delusion and all the dishonesties won't work any more. These can be holy moments, moments when we come to the end of self and turn to God.

Robert Frost has written:

They cannot scare me with their empty spaces between stars,
On stars where no human race is.

I have it in me so much nearer home to scare myself
With my own desert places.

Wrestling with God

In those twenty years of separation, Esau has become a gracious man, quick to forgive, but Jacob doesn't know that.
We read in Proverbs 28:1, "The wicked flee when no man
pursueth" (KJV). Jacob is making all these elaborate plans
to escape his brother's wrath because he is so guilty. He is
the enemy, not his brother. At the brook Jabbok, Jacob falls
into the hands of the living God. There is a struggle, one
that lasts all night. Perhaps you've had that experience of
wrestling all night with God. You may have lain awake, as
I have, because of something you have done or wished you
had done—you're tossing and turning and trying to make
peace with God in those shabby places of your life.

Twenty years before, Jacob had met God at a place called
Bethel (meaning "the house of God") in a very different
encounter from this one at Peniel by the brook Jabbok. We
could compare the Bethel encounter with being at a senior
high retreat, where in the glow of the campfire on the last
night, we're overwhelmed by the reality of God. We swear
to serve Him, and we feel wonderfully confident that a long
and problem-free life lies ahead. Bethel was that sort of high
moment for Jacob. But at Peniel, twenty years later, his life
is falling apart and he is faced with the harsh reality of who
he is and what he has done, and he wrestles with God and
is wounded. The encounter with God at Peniel, unlike the
one at Bethel, is a crippling one.

Every time we meet God, we are different and He is different. Life is never static. Every encounter between the same
two people, even within long-term relationships, is different.
You can't step in the river at the same place twice; the river
is forever moving. At Bethel, God reassured Jacob and promised to bless him. At Peniel, a battle is waged and Jacob is

wounded. Lloyd Ogilvie, pastor of the First Presbyterian Church of Hollywood, and an old friend, tells about one of the turning points in his life as a young theological student in Scotland. He was studying under one of the great minds and hearts of our time, James Stewart. After class one day, Lloyd stayed to ask Dr. Stewart some questions about preaching and pastoring. At one point, Dr. Stewart leaned across his desk and said, "Do you know what you need to do, Mr. Ogilvie? You need to die!" Lloyd said he knew exactly what Stewart meant. He didn't need more theology or more biblical studies. "Something had to die in me before God could have His way with me."

Something in Jacob died at Peniel. God may wound us in that way but we read in the New Testament, "My strength is made perfect in weakness." And Jacob was more complete lame than when he was whole. Jacob's lameness served another important purpose. He could never say, "Was that just a dream I had beside the brook Jabbok? Did God really meet me there?" For the rest of his life, the limp was a constant reminder of God's intervention in his life.

But after the struggle in which he was wounded, Jacob demands a blessing. Imagine prevailing against God! What a tough old codger Jacob was. God could not defeat him. Jacob says, "I will not let You go unless You bless me." It seems like effrontery, doesn't it? Do we dare say, "God, I demand that You bless me?" I believe we do. I love the forthrightness of Jacob's request. He did not say, "Bless me— if it be Thy will." There was no such hedging. We believe it is God's nature to bless—that it is always His will. We can pray for healing, certain that God always wills it. There may be reasons why it does not happen, but God wills it. I'd be curious to know exactly what Jacob wanted when he asked for a blessing. He may have wanted more money, more flocks. He may have wanted simply to have his life spared. I'd like to think that he was smart enough *not* to tell God how to bless him, that he demanded an open-ended blessing.

To *demand* what God *wants* to give us is not arrogant.

We might think of it in these terms. Suppose one of your children was addicted to drugs or flunking out of school. If that child came to you demanding help to get his or her life straightened out, demanding support to go to school and start again, what would you say? "No way, kid, you blew it." Of course not. That's not the kind of blessing we parents are waiting to give. If we, with all our weaknesses, want to bless our children, how much more does God want to bless us! In this meeting at Peniel, Jacob understood the heart of God and when he demanded a blessing he got it.

A Time of Confession

The blessing he receives is threefold. First of all, it involves a confession. To begin the blessing, God asks, "What is your name?" We can be certain God already knew Jacob's name. It's important for Jacob to tell God his name, since it literally means "Supplanter" or "Cheat" and he and God both know how he has lived up to this name with his father, his brother, and his father-in-law. Jacob, in answering this one question, owns up to who he is and what he's been and done.

A lot of us have been given names which needed either living up to or living down. We have been called beautiful or ugly, dumb or smart, spunky or spineless, wimp or bully. Those names come from all sorts of sources, from parents, spouses, peer groups. Recently, I read about Mary K. Trimble, the young daughter of Congressman Trimble from Virginia who at age five was trying to preserve her own identity in the midst of her father's political campaign. Tired of having strangers say, "You must be Congressman Trimble's daughter" she asked her mother how to handle this problem. "Tell them no, that's not true," advised her mother, "that you are Mary K. Trimble." Shortly after that, the inevitable question was put to her by the mayor of Newport News, Virginia. "Aren't you Congressman Trimble's daughter?" "No," said

Mary, "my mother says that's not true." But the encouraging part of the story is that even at age five, Mary was not letting anybody hang a label on her.

A Time of Assurance

Having confessed his name, Jacob receives a new one from God. Instead of being a "Supplanter," his new name is Israel, which means "God rules." This is the heart of conversion. Conversion is simply that turnabout time in your life when you surrender to God and allow Him to make you who you were when He first thought of you. You may have strayed a long way from His original intention, but an encounter with God at such a moment of truth can be the means of finding your true self and true identity.

A member of our congregation was severely handicapped and suffered from many illnesses. She had been on pain-killing drugs for years and doctors had told her that she would be dependent on those drugs for the rest of her life. She didn't believe that. One day she came to a healing service at our church and went forward for the laying on of hands by the elders. She has since kicked all these drugs and is getting well. She said, "I refused to accept the name given me by doctors—hopeless." She is now back at school, making straight A's, and is a competitive athlete.

A young man very dear to me told me about an experience he had last year. He'd had a terrible fight with the girl he thought he was going to marry. The relationship ended with all sorts of bitter recriminations. In the two-hour drive back to his home, this young man was blinded by tears and in despair. A hitchhiker appeared along the road and my friend picked him up. It turned out that the hitchhiker had just been released from prison and was trying to overcome alcoholism. As they drove along, this ex-prisoner began talking about Jesus and the power of God to enable new beginnings. My young friend said, "All of a sudden the car seemed filled with light and God was there." Two hours later, he arrived back home a different person. This girl with whom he had been so obsessed seemed almost unimportant. Even his career didn't seem to matter very much compared to God and His plan and purposes. The pain was gone. This kind of life-changing encounter still happens and a new identity results. Abram had his name changed to Abraham. Simon became Peter. Saul became Paul. Joseph was renamed Barnabas, "son of encouragement," by the early church.

A Time to Trust

The third part of the blessing underscores the walk of faith. Jacob, now named Israel, asks his adversary, "What is your name?" He is told, in essence, that it is none of his business. We don't need to know everything there is to know about God. The important thing is to meet Him, to trust Him, to put your hand in His. Knowing all about God is not the same as trusting your life to Him in your day-by-day walk.

Imagine for a moment that you have come upon a little boy lost and crying in some large department store. Suppose you said to him, "Please don't cry. I know who you are, and I know where you live. I'll give you some directions for getting there. In fact, I'll draw a map showing how to get there on the bus, and I'll stake you to the bus fare." I have a hunch that, in spite of all these offers of help, he would still be crying and wailing, "I'm lost, I'm lost." If, however, his mother should appear at that moment, he would stop crying immediately, put his hand in hers with perfect assurance that she would take him home. Maps aren't much help to somebody who is lost. Neither are plans of salvation and detailed theologies. We need to meet the living God so that He can take us home.

I heard about some mice who lived in the bottom of a piano. From time to time they'd hear stirring piano music and they loved it, picturing some invisible musician who filled their lives with beauty. One day a scientifically minded mouse climbed up from the bottom of the piano to find out more about this phenomenon. He came back with the news, "It's all done with taut wires and little hammers." The mice were astonished. "All wires and hammers?" Thereafter, whenever the music played, they were indifferent. "It's all wires and hammers," they would say. Science and theology can't put you in touch with the living God. They may explain certain things for us, but God says to us, as to Jacob, "You don't have to know all about Me. You have to trust Me and walk by faith."

The result of Jacob's life-changing night was that he was reconciled to Esau. Esau came out to meet Jacob with over-whelming and unexpected graciousness. Jacob's gifts were unimportant, he told him. He was just glad to have him back. Jacob was still less than honest with his brother, leading him to believe he would follow him to Seir, when actually he had no intention of doing so. But, they were reconciled. When you fall into the hands of the living God and are blessed and transformed and begin the faith walk, reconciliation is the next step. Jesus' last prayer on the night of His betrayal was that we might all be one. "He who does not love his brother whom he has seen, cannot love God whom he has not seen" (1 John 4:20). Proof that you love God is that you love your brother.

Believe that God has it in mind to bless you extraordinarily. Perhaps He has already. Jacob was rich and well and happy but, in a life-threatening situation, he demanded God's bless-ing and received forgiveness, new identity, and reconciliation with his brother. Whenever we come to the end of our own resources, those are times when wrestling with God takes place. Next time that happens, I urge you to demand your blessings.

16. A Cure for the "If Onlys"

There are two kinds of fools, someone observed. One says, "This is old, therefore it is good," and the other, "This is new, therefore it is better." We all have a tendency to live life in the past or in the future, but faith can be exercised only in the now. In the person of the Holy Spirit, God is dealing with us in the now. The Apostle Paul writes in Romans 8:28, "We know that in everything God works for good with those who love him who are called according to his purpose." It is easier, in retrospect, to see the truth of that. And we may believe it as we consider the future. But somehow, it's harder to see God working for good in the now, in the particular situations and circumstances we are grappling with at this moment. Nevertheless, the only opportunity to apply our faith is in the now. If we trust God with the present, the past is gone and the future assured.

Family Politics

Genesis 37 deals with the politics of the family. It's a clinical study of a kid named Joe and it is a contemporary tale about what life is and has always been like in families. Joe is the kind of kid you love to hate. Joe was a tattler and a braggart. He was pop's favorite, indulged and arrogant. Reading about him, I'm reminded of some of the kids I've known that I have loved to hate. Some friends of ours had a kid like that. In his pre-teen years he was the worst kid I ever saw. When these friends came for a visit, this kid could turn the house into a disaster area in no time. He managed to break a good many of our children's toys and even got into my books and papers. He was still a terror, even when he was old enough to know better. Through all this mayhem, his parents' only comment was, "Isn't he cute?" He wasn't cute. He was a little monster. I'm sure you can think of at least one child like that.

The problems of the family are unavoidable, even for the rich and famous. David Kennedy, one of that famous Kennedy tribe, died as a result of a drug overdose. An in-depth story about this young man tells us that he was the runt of the litter in a family that prizes excellence and athletic achievement. Unable to compete in those areas, he turned to less wholesome pursuits. One newspaper reported: "Some friend of his, adept in modern therapies, called him the designated sick one who made the others in the family seem normal." True or not, David's tragic story is one that points up the whole idea of the politics of the family.

The story of Joseph and his brethren is a story of love and hate, of betrayal and attempted murder, and of a father's grief. But, it's also the story of the hidden call of God. We believe in a God who can still be at work when all He has created seems to have gone wrong. We find God working out His destiny for Joseph in spite of the politics of the family. He is still the Creator-friend whose love pursues us in every circumstance.

The family we have been reading about in these chapters of Genesis is not exactly your typical nuclear family. While there is just one father, there are two wives and two concubines. At the time of these events, Leah is the only wife. Joseph's mother, Jacob's beloved Rachel, died when the youngest, Benjamin, was born. At any rate, the family is now made up of Jacob, the three mothers, twelve sons, and one daughter—just an ordinary family. And Joe is the darling.

The Bible and indeed life itself is full of that kind of favoritism in the family. One child has the capacity to delight the parents. Wrath may come down on the other children for fairly minor infractions while the crimes of the blessed child are overlooked and minimized. The Bible sets up this situation in the story of Cain and Abel. There's also the New Testament story of the Prodigal Son and the older brother. The Prodigal was the blessed child. "Daddy, give me my inheritance. I don't need you any more. See you around." Off he goes, while the elder brother stays home and works the farm, hoping some day to earn the father's blessing, or at least, a party. I'm sure you've witnessed this sad drama in lots of families. You walk into a home that seems almost a shrine, full of one child's trophies with no indication that the others have accomplished anything at all. We feel embarrassed and yet the parents are totally unaware of their partisanism. As a parent, if you're unsure about who the blessed child is in your family, just ask your kids. I promise you, they'll know.

Joseph is this kind of blessed and pampered child, perhaps because he was the first child born to Rachel. When Jacob buried Rachel, he buried his heart with her. She was his great love and for her he had served his father-in-law fourteen long years. Perhaps Joseph was especially beloved because he was a reminder of that love and also a child of Jacob's old age. Jacob shows the same favoritism to Joseph that his mother showed him and which became the cause of his alienation from his father and his brother. The Bible says, "The sins of the parents are visited upon the children unto the third and fourth generations." We tend to repeat the same stupid mistakes our parents made, unless God's grace crashes through at some point and breaks the chain.

The story begins when Joseph's father gives him a long-sleeved coat, which, in those days, was a royal garment, a garment for somebody who wasn't expected to work. Imagine. There are ten working brothers (Benjamin is still too young to be in the field) and Joseph appears in this long-sleeved coat in which he can do no chores. The other ten have short-sleeved coats (the Old Testament equivalent of bib overalls) which provide freedom of arm movement in their labors. Of course, they hate this non-worker in his royal garment. They hate him because he's a tattler, a braggart, and the favorite, and they conspire to murder him. The oldest brother, Reuben, who is responsible for the whole group, thwarts the first attempt. They compromise by casting Joseph into a pit from which Reuben intends later to rescue him. But meanwhile, a caravan comes by and the brothers sell Joseph to the Ishmaelites, who take him to Egypt as a slave.

Next, the brothers plot to deceive their father. They bring him back Joseph's bloody garment and indicate that some wild beast has devoured him. Jacob is inconsolable. On hearing this news, he's plunged into a timeless sorrow and drops out of life. You may have known people who've done that or perhaps you've been there yourself. A beloved wife or husband or child dies, and nothing is ever the same again. The grieving party withdraws and becomes almost a non-person.

With monumental hypocrisy, the sons who have caused this grief attempt to comfort their father. Have you ever wondered how their guilty secret affected family life in the ensuing years? We can imagine the mistrust building between them as they realize that if one of them confesses what really happened, they all will be exposed. The certain result of their crime of passion is loneliness and separation. The erosion of the whole family relationship is inevitable.

Belated Regrets

Life is full of foolish decisions—for you, for me, for this family. They did things for which they were eternally sorry. A good many of life's sorrows are not the result of unhappy circumstances. They come from the "if onlys"—the desperate wish that we had done or said something other than what we did do or say, corporately as a nation or group, or personally and individually.

An investigation into the sinking of the *Titanic* has been under way for more than fifty years. The *Titanic,* you may remember, the first "unsinkable" ship, rammed into an iceberg on its maiden voyage, and fifteen hundred passengers were drowned. The verdict of this lengthy investigation was that the whole tragedy is still to be considered an act of God. However, records indicate that the naval authorities in England permitted the *Titanic* to sail with only sixteen lifeboats aboard, just enough for the crew, whereas the law required forty-eight lifeboats. With the proper complement of lifeboats, perhaps no lives would have been lost. We can only assume that someone made that particular decision, and, instead of taking responsibility for it, the culpability was shifted to God. This particular "act of God" might more aptly be labeled an "if only."

I heard about a father who was asked to sign his son's report card, full of failing grades. The dad did so with an X. "Why did you do that, Dad?" asked his son. His dad replied, "I don't want the teacher to think someone with grades like that has a father who can read and write." Those of us with children sometimes give ourselves poor grades in parenting and are full of regrets for all the things we did or did not do. In his grief, Jacob must have had some "if onlys." "Why did I send Joseph out all alone to find his brothers?" Jacob may even have regretted some of his unwise behavior toward Joseph that created such enmity with his brothers.

Joseph too must have suffered some "if onlys." Certainly, while he was down in that dry well, he must have reflected on how stupid he had been to alienate his brothers with his bragging and tattling and boasting. He sat in the well for many hours, perhaps realizing too late that he had not behaved very wisely toward his brothers. "If only" he had acted more humbly and lovingly.

And surely Reuben had his "if onlys." He should have known better than to expect responsible behavior from his younger brothers who were his charges. "If only I had interfered," he may have said; "if only I could tell my father the truth. If only there were some way to get Joseph back."

We all have our "if onlys." If only I had told the IRS the truth; if only I had not betrayed the person I love most; if only I had not told that lie in the office or in my neighborhood; if only I had worked harder at school; if only I hadn't been a party to vicious gossip. The "if onlys" are there for all of us. They are part of the human condition.

A few months ago, a friend of mine had an accident on the freeway. His car was sideswiped by a sports car driven by an attractive young woman. Neither party was hurt, but the other driver was distraught. "This is a brand new car. My husband just bought it for me. He'll be heartbroken." Eventually, the police came and, in the process of exchanging registration and insurance papers, a note fell out of the glove compartment of the young woman's car. It was written by her husband and this was the message: "Darling, if you ever need to use these, remember that it's you I love and not the car." What foresight—to reassure someone you love at a time when they need that reassurance the most. When I heard the story, I thought to myself, "If only I were thoughtful enough to do something like that."

God's Sovereignty

The only cure for the "if onlys" is to believe in the sovereignty of God. The hidden call of God makes allowances for the "if onlys." That's the wonder of Joseph's story. The Bible rubs our noses into the politics of the family and the ugliness of life, and yet in it all God is present and in control and has a destiny for us as He did for Joseph. A life of faith is not free of "if onlys." They are inevitable. We will have regrets about what we did or didn't do, but God is big enough to use those as building blocks in our lives.

Beyond the regrets that plague us about our own actions or lack of them, there are those regrets we feel about things beyond our control, injustices perpetrated by society, or our families. But God can be at work even in those. Someone wrote:

> Cripple him and you have a Sir Walter Scott.
> Put him in prison and you have a John Bunyan.
> Bury him in snow at Valley Forge and you have a George
>   Washington.
> Have him born in abject poverty and you have an Abraham
>   Lincoln.
> Goad him with bitter racial prejudice and you have a Disraeli.
> Afflict him with asthma as a boy and you have a Theodore
>   Roosevelt.
> Stab him with rheumatic pain until he cannot sleep without
>   an opiate and you have a Charles Steinmetz.
> Make him black of slave parents and sell him for the price
>   of a fair to average horse and you have a George
>   Washington Carver.

Peter and Judas both loved Jesus and both betrayed Him. Both must have endured poignant "if onlys." Peter confessed his and went on to be the great shepherd while Judas, unable to forgive himself, took his life.

I want you to walk with me into the home of a new mother. She asks you to come in while she bathes the baby. The kitchen looks like a disaster area. The baby is in the bathinette. There's water all over the floor. There is cereal everywhere, even up the wall. The sink is full of eggshells and burnt toast and dirty dishes. In the midst of this mess, she catches you looking at a blue ribbon over the sink on which hangs a Phi Beta Kappa key. "Ah, you noticed," she says. "I hung it there to remind myself that if I was smart enough to get

that, I'm smart enough to get myself out of this present mess."
We may not all be Phi Beta Kappas, but God is big enough
to use even the mess we're in and even the "if onlys." As
we commit our lives to Him, our talents, abilities, gifts, and
all we have and are, He can take even the "if onlys" and
use them for good as He works out our personal destiny.

The New Testament continues the great theme begun in
Genesis. In Romans 8 we read: ". . . Who shall separate
us from the love of Christ? Shall tribulation, or distress, or
persecution, or famine, or nakedness, or peril, or sword?
. . . No, in all these things we are more than conquerors
through him who loved us. For I am sure that neither death,
nor life, nor angels, nor principalities, nor things present,
nor things to come, nor powers, nor height, nor depth, nor
anything else in all creation, will be able to separate us from
the love of God in Christ Jesus our Lord."

17. Where Is God When You Need Him?

Genesis 39 and 40

Joseph's story is the stuff of a good many parents' dreams—the transformation of an arrogant, self-centered brat into a gracious and gifted human being who blesses all those who come into contact with him. Isn't that exactly what we want for all our problem kids?

In the Dark Ages, people dreamed of finding a "philosopher's stone" which would transform base metals like lead into gold. But God's philosopher's stone, the gift of faith, is even more desirable. With it, the base substances of our lives are transformed into that which is precious and valuable.

Someone has said that the hardness of God is kinder than the softness of men. Joseph's father would never have chosen for him the circumstances which brought him to Egypt. God is not the author of the crimes and injustices which have brought Joseph to this place, but He allowed it all to happen. Yet in the crucible of real life—for Joseph that meant slavery, servitude, and prison—Joseph has the gift of faith whereby the lead of his life is transformed into gold as he becomes Egypt's prime minister and ultimately the savior of the whole nation and much of the world beyond.

Triumphs and Catastrophes

To begin with, let's review all the unfortunate events of Joseph's early life. He is sold into slavery not by his enemies, but by his own brothers, which means his blood brothers *were* his enemies. *Where is God when you need Him?* Joseph must have asked. Next, he lands a prestigious job, considering that he is a mere slave. He becomes the honored steward of his master's house, in charge of everything with no privileges withheld. He loses that job simply because he is a man of faith and integrity and honor. *Where is God when you need Him?* The upshot is that he is sentenced to prison on trumped-up charges. *Where is God when you need Him?* By interpreting dreams, he blesses the jailer and some of his fellow-prisoners, one of whom is the king's butler. The butler promises, "When I get out of here I'm going to remember you." Nevertheless, on his release, he promptly forgets all about Joseph, who remains in prison another two years. *Where is God when you need Him?*

The story of the butler is a familiar one. The butler committed no crime against Joseph. He simply used him and his wisdom and moved on without a backward glance. Joseph suffered two more years through the sin of omission rather than commission. Reading about this incident jogged my own memory. I began to think of the people who blessed me at some point in my life and whom I've since forgotten. I've done them no evil. I just haven't remembered them with a letter, a phone call, something to indicate my appreciation for the fact that they were there with a helping hand or an encouraging word when I needed it. I'm sure you can think of people like that from your past—a teacher, neighbor, friend, relative. The butler's story is a reminder to us all to do a better job of remembering those special people who have blessed us along the journey.

The Bible, over and over again, underscores the unfairness

of life. Joseph, through no fault of his own, finds himself first a slave and then a prisoner. As we read about the Apostle Paul's journey to Rome, the voyage is perilous, one of the ships he boards runs aground and is wrecked. Even though an angel of the Lord has assured Paul he is to appear before Caesar in Rome, throughout the many stages of the voyage we read that "the winds were against us." We may be off on God's business, trying our best to serve Him, and yet the winds are against us.

I wonder if you can identify this person before I reveal who it is. At age nine his mother died. At age twenty-two he lost his job as a store clerk. He wanted to go to law school, but his education wasn't adequate. At twenty-three he went into debt to become a partner in a small store. At twenty-six his business partner died leaving him with a huge debt that took years to repay. At twenty-eight, he asked the girl he had been courting for four years to marry him, and she said no. At thirty-seven, on his third try, he was elected to Congress, but two years later he failed to be re-elected. At forty-five he lost the Senate race. At forty-seven he was defeated as a vice-presidential candidate. At forty-nine he again ran for the Senate and again he lost. All of that happened to Abraham Lincoln. At last, at fifty-one, he was elected President of the United States and is revered as one of our greatest presidents. People like Lincoln are a reminder that hardships and obstacles need not prevent achievement of our eventual destinies.

All of us have those times when we wonder, *Where is God when you need Him?* If we have the gift of faith, we know the answer. He is there with us in all the hardness and unfairness of life. God does not always protect us from trouble, but He is in it with us. Our faith in those times is the philosopher's stone that turns our despair into hope, our anxieties to trust.

Joseph's adventures in Egypt begin in Genesis 39. In both verses 2 and 21 of that chapter, we read, "The Lord was with Joseph." In the midst of this see-saw of success and disgrace, privilege and prison, "The Lord showed him steadfast love and gave him favor."

Resisting Temptation

Faith for Joseph meant sticking to his principles in spite of temptation. In his very first job, he is trusted by his employer, Potiphar, and given all sorts of powers and responsibilities. Potiphar's wife is attracted to him and tries to seduce him. Joseph refuses to betray his employer. We can be fairly certain that this young man, away from home and lonely and in his full manhood, is sorely tempted by this beautiful woman who says she's just got to have him. But there's a difference between temptation and sin. Joseph, understanding what is at stake, will not give in to her desires.

Satan is called the father of lies, and one of his lies is that illicit sex is OK. It's fun; you deserve it; enjoy, he says. The message comes through to us subtly—and not so subtly— by means of all sorts of vehicles including slick magazines and sophisticated movies. Joseph understands that Mrs. Potiphar is suggesting not just a pleasurable diversion, but adultery. To acquiesce would be a sin against his master, the lady, and himself. Beyond that, there is his duty to God. He may be a slave, but he is serving God, and to give in to these attempts at seduction would be a sin against Him. Faith for Joseph means resisting temptation not only for his own sake and his employer's, but most of all, because he belongs to God.

Employing a clever ruse, Mrs. Potiphar sets the stage so that it appears Joseph has seduced her, and Joseph is charged with adultery. Though this was an offense punishable by death in both Israelite and Egyptian law, he was sentenced to prison instead. We're not sure how or why that came about. Perhaps Potiphar was too fond of Joseph to press for the death penalty. It's even possible that he knew his wife's weaknesses and guessed she wasn't as innocent in all this as she claimed. For whatever reason, Joseph's life is spared.

In chapter 40 we read about the occasion we touched on earlier where Joseph interprets dreams for two fellow-prisoners, a butler and a baker, formerly employed by the Pharaoh. There were all sorts of people in those times, as there are today, who would interpret dreams for you. Some were charlatans and some were reputable. Today, dreams are given Freudian or Gestalt interpretation, or you can interpret your own dreams with the help of any number of books about dreams. Joseph's method is simpler. He says, "Do not interpretations belong to God? Tell them [your dreams] to me." Over and over again, even though his circumstances are dismal, unfair, and seemingly hopeless, Joseph affirms that God is with him.

Practicing God's Presence

Joseph bet his life on God's presence and that's what faith is. I received a letter recently from a young man who was attempting to do that.

Dear Bruce:

. . . Two years ago, shortly after I moved to the U. District to attend the University of Washington, I was suffering a mean loneliness. So many bad things were happening to me. I felt no acceptance within most churches. I hardly had any real friends. My studies were oppressive. I had just had surgery for minor cancer with a prospect of periodic recurrences the rest of my life. My financial situation was shaky. My family and acquaintances only used me and didn't seem to have much real interest in me. I was without hope. I could have written a sequel to Ecclesiastes.

I came to your church an angry young man. Then, you suggested an experiment. "Thank God for every experience He has given us." It was a ludicrous idea. Not only was I not thankful, but God would punish me again, this time for hypocrisy. As I left the church, smiling politely to the ushers, I was inwardly a bitter stew of sarcasm, resentment, and unbelief. I immediately tried the experiment. The first few days I thanked God without much enthusiasm. Gradually, I started to see some reasons for the things I was thanking Him for. I had to think of something so I wouldn't feel like a perfect fool. I continued the experiment beyond thirty days.

Two years later I'm still thanking Him. The experiment has become a philosophy. My life is quite different now. I've still got tremendous challenges in my life, but I see them now as purposeful. Sometimes they're even fun, and I look at them sideways. In the final analysis, I see, perhaps, the major point. My problems were designed to bring me to God so that I could experience His strength, peace, and love. I've been healed. Keep telling your people to thank Him. It's a noble idea. Thanks.

Where is God when you need Him? He's right there with us. We can bet our lives on it. It may be true the people you counted on have forgotten you, as the butler at first forgot Joseph, but God has not. We can believe with certainty that God is there when we need Him, but what about the reverse of that?

The Kind of Person God Needs

Where are you when God needs you? God can use you in the place or circumstances you are in right now just as He did Joseph. Everybody and everything around Joseph flourished. Potiphar was blessed and his land and houses prospered. The jailer was blessed and put the whole prison under Joseph's management. The prisoners were blessed. Joseph was the kind of chief executive every corporation tries to hire.

Let's consider some of Joseph's attributes. First of all, Joseph was relational. He had found favor with the keeper of the prison and been put in charge of these two high-ranking prisoners from Pharaoh's court. In Genesis 40:6–8 we read:

"When Joseph came to them in the morning and saw them, they were troubled. So he asked Pharaoh's officers who were with him in custody in his master's house, 'Why are your faces downcast today?' They said to him, 'We have had dreams, and there is no one to interpret them.' And Joseph said to them, 'Do not interpretations belong to God? Tell them to me, I pray you.' "

Joseph begins the conversation by expressing concern that they seemed depressed. A relational person is a gracious person, someone who has the ability to be on the other person's agenda. Joseph might have entered their cell full of his own problems, and he had plenty of those. "Have I told you about how unfairly I've been treated? Listen, I am innocent and I was wrongly charged. I may never get out of here." He might have used his position to go from prisoner to prisoner, complaining about what a bad rap he'd gotten. Instead, this young man, imprisoned unfairly, comes into the cell and observes them carefully and notices they are troubled. Then he asks them a question which, translated in the vernacular, could be, "What's the problem?" He is concerned for them and available to help. Joseph was sensitive. He asked how they were doing and listened to them, all of which is not too unlike love. To begin with, then, we find that Joseph was gracious and loving; he listened a lot and he wanted to help. In other words, he was relational.

David Burns, a medical doctor and professor of psychiatry at the University of Pennsylvania, says: "The biggest mistake you can make in trying to talk convincingly is to put your highest priority on expressing *your* ideas and feelings. What most people really want is to be *listened* to, *respected,* and *understood.* The moment people see that they are being understood, they become more motivated to understand *your* point of view." That's a good thing to remember as we try to witness to someone else about our faith. We want to bless them as Joseph did.

Recently my wife went to do her grocery shopping in a

supermarket she hadn't visited before. She came home in a particularly expansive mood. "I just met the young man who's going to be the next manager of that store," she reported. "He was at the checkout counter, and when I came through, he asked all about me. 'Are you new here? Who are you? Where do you live? I hope we can help you.' I felt so cared for. That young man has a future." I'm sure that's the kind of person who will manage the whole chain someday. There are all too few people like Joseph, who are on the other person's agenda.

Where are you when God needs you? It is not enough to be relational. Are you *reliable?* Joseph was. Surely, he must have been tempted by Potiphar's wife, but he was unseduceable. Because he belonged to God, he couldn't do what he would have enjoyed doing. He was morally and sexually pure. On the other hand, we read in Genesis about Adam and Eve giving in to temptation. God had given them dominion over the whole creation. There was just one thing they were not to do, one tree the fruit of which was forbidden. Satan, through the serpent, convinced them that they deserved it all and they believed him. Joseph understood that giving in to temptation meant betraying himself and his employer and turning his back on God. In spite of all Mrs. Potiphar's wiles, he was unseduceable.

Joseph was also *resourceful.* Ann Landers, one of our country's resident theologians, says: "Opportunity is usually disguised as hard work, so most people don't recognize it." Joseph, as an act of faith, gave his employers all he had. Perhaps the jobs—household steward and prison manager—weren't all that desirable, but that's where God had placed him. I'd like to think he said, "Until God gives me a better job, I'm going to give this one my best shot." I heard about a sign posted on an employees' bulletin board that warned: "Employees that are not fired with enthusiasm will be fired with enthusiasm." Every firm is looking for that person who will take the job in hand and do it as unto the Lord. Joseph succeeded in both jobs because he did just that. He made the most of his unfortunate situation.

I read a story recently about Eddie Rickenbacker's life which suggested he was a similar kind of person. He was, of course, the famous race car driver and number one flying ace in World War I who went on to found Eastern Airlines. Eddie Rickenbacker was born in 1890 in Columbus, Ohio. He was the third of eight children and quit school at age eleven to help support the family. He went to work immediately for $3.50 a week. He took a night correspondence course in automotive mechanics and, when he felt he had mastered the course, he went to call on a local automotive company where he caught the attention of one of the owners.

"What are you doing here?" asked the employer.

Rickenbacker said, "I just thought I'd tell you I'm coming to work here tomorrow morning."

"Who hired you?"

"Nobody," said Rickenbacker, "but if you think I'm not worth hiring, you can fire me."

Sure enough, the next morning he reported for work. He noticed some iron filings and grease on the floor, so he found a shovel and broom and cleaned the place up. He went from job to job, each time making himself invaluable. It wasn't long before he convinced his employers they couldn't run that business without him. That's the Joseph quality of resourcefulness.

Where is God when you need Him—when life is unjust and unfair, as it is for all of us sometimes? He's there with us. But perhaps we all need to think more about where we are when God needs *us*. By accident or divine will, we are right now in a place of responsibility. We can serve God in that place when we are, like Joseph, relational, reliable, and resourceful. And that is the result of knowing that we are never alone—we have a Friend.

18. The Creative Dimension

Genesis 41

When I preached on creativity about a year or so ago, it also happened to be Mother's Day. I was struck by the compatibility of my subject with the observance of that highly sentimental holiday. Each of us has been given the gift of life by our mother and in that sense, she is the instrument of God's creativity. And for most of us, she is usually the first person to begin to call forth our creative capacities.

Beginning at birth, mothers teach us important skills that keep us from starving to death. When we are weaned from the breast or bottle, mothers show us how to keep the food in our mouths instead of spraying it across the room or dribbling it down our chins. They introduce us to a more creative way of disposing of our waste than soiling a diaper. They teach us to smile, to say words, and eventually to express ourselves artistically with the crayons and paints and all sorts of materials they provide. They teach us how to handle life— how to behave at a birthday party, how to handle a bully, how to get through a tough course in school. Mothers, at their best, are God-like. They give life and they call forth creativity.

I was having dinner recently with two bishops of the diocese of Pittsburgh and their wives. I sat next to Dora Stevenson, the wife of the retired bishop. She revealed some

interesting history. "You know my maiden name was Queer.
That was my father's name. My mother's maiden name was
Veri. I am the product of a Veri Queer union." My response
was, "Aren't we all?" There is nobody else exactly like your
mother and your father. We are all the products of a very
queer (perhaps *unique* is a better word) union—those people
God has used to give us life.

God is, of course, *the* Creator and it seems to me the story
we find in Genesis 41 focuses on that dimension of God.
Thirteen years have elapsed since Joseph's betrayal by his
brothers. This young man who came to Egypt as a slave becomes, eventually, the number two person in the known
world. He is second in command to Egypt's Pharaoh, the
most powerful person of his time. In those years, two sons
were born to Joseph. The first is named Manasseh, meaning
"God has made me forget all my hardships and all my father's
house." The name was symbolic of Joseph's decision to forgive and forget. The second son is named Aphrim, which
means "God has made me fruitful in the land of my affliction."

A Divine Warning

Joseph's rise to power begins when Pharaoh has a dream.
It is a dream given to save the lives of many, in fact, the
whole civilized world, because the coming famine would be
so widespread. We learn from just this small incident that
God is a friend who wants good things for all those He
has created. God loves the world, believers and nonbelievers,
and He gives Pharaoh a dream to warn him of the devastation
to come in order that many may be saved.

We already know that Joseph believes in dreams and has
interpreted dreams for others. He believes in a God who is
speaking in those dreams. When he is asked to interpret Pharaoh's dream, his response is a humble one. We could paraphrase it like this: "I can't do this. I have no secret powers,
but I serve a God who will tell me what the dream means."

Usually, those who seem chosen by God to be His special messengers have that kind of humility. They are not arrogant know-it-alls but those who say, "I have no special power, but God is able." Billy Graham, who is perhaps the number one spokesman for the Christian faith in the world, has that kind of humility. He prefers to give God the credit for the success of his ministry and to admit that his own abilities are not all that unusual. Joseph is like that.

Joseph not only interprets the dream but he suggests a course of action requiring some spiritual entrepreneurship. He convinces Pharaoh that if he can find someone to make the proper preparations, many lives will be saved. Then, with a willingness to risk that we admire, he asks Pharaoh to bet on his interpretation of the dream and to store food for the next seven years. Such a scheme must have seemed foolhardy and unnecessary when the land was productive and storehouses bulging. Pharaoh makes what must have been a difficult decision. He decides to follow Joseph's advice at the risk of being stuck with warehouses of food and grain.

In essence, Joseph is asking Pharaoh to trust him for the next seven years, during which all this hoarding of food will look idiotic. The contract between Pharaoh and Joseph amounts to long-term obedience and long-term risk. God, through Joseph, is bringing a creative solution to what will be a worldwide problem in just seven years.

By means of the dream, Joseph taps into God's creativity. That is possible for all of us. I think God wants to give us this kind of creative solution to all sorts of human problems. We are made in the image of God and we are the only animals that we know of in the world, perhaps in the cosmos, with the capacity to create. We are able to study situations and problems and come up with solutions. We can write poetry and music, build bridges and buildings, and be a part of God's creative process of saving and ennobling and enriching life. To do and be less than that is sin because that's what being God-like, created in His image, is all about.

Old Problems, New Solutions

If that's true, then doing business as usual, living life by rote, is sinful. We stifle God's creativity within us when we repeat forever the skills and methods handed down by parents and teachers. To play out the script you were given with no deviation is, to me, a more serious sin than kicking the dog and being grouchy at home or cutting corners at work. In Acts 2, the prophecy of the Old Testament prophet Joel is fulfilled and God pours out His spirit on all people. The young, the old, men and women, Joel had said, would all dream dreams and have visions. God wants to give us those dreams and visions in order that we might bring fresh solutions to old problems and find new ways to bless and help the hungry and hurting people of the world. Each of us has that capacity and it is a sin not to exercise it.

David Ogilvy, the founder of Ogilvy, Benson, and Mather, one of the great advertising firms of our time, says that "the majority of businessmen are incapable of original thought because they are unable to escape the tyranny of reason." J. Willard Marriott, of the Marriott hotel chain, says, "I've never been satisfied with anything we've ever built. I've felt that dissatisfaction is the basis for progress. When we become satisfied in business we become obsolete." Much earlier on, Carlyle said, "Every noble work is at first impossible."

By faith, we begin an impossible task because we think God is in it. Seven years went by before Joseph could be certain his vision was really authentic and that's a long time to trust. A couple in our church have been missionaries to the Masai tribe in Kenya for fifteen years. They attempted an impossible task. Because of drought and reapportionment of land, these African nomads can no longer survive by roaming the plains, herding cattle. Denny and Jeanne Grindall had a vision to teach these people to settle in one place, to create reliable sources of water and learn to farm. Everybody said it was impossible. The Masai were doomed to extinction.

There is no water in the dry Rift Valley where they live and furthermore, these proud cattle owners would never consent to dig in the ground and grow vegetables, let alone eat them. The Grindalls believed God loved the Masai and had a better way for their African brothers and sisters to live. They have built dams and windmills which provide water for gardens. They built a model village with houses made of concrete instead of the traditional dung huts which attract flies and disease. They followed their vision in faith.

The philosopher M. N. Tyrell said that there are two kinds of problems, convergent and divergent. Convergent problems are those that can be solved by logical thought process. Divergent problems can only be solved by living and dreaming. You can't think your way through them. The tragedy of our technological age, according to Tyrell, is that we are trying to solve most of the world's problems with convergent thinking, which can't be done. Instead, we've got to live and dream our way into more solutions.

The Author of Dreams

Einstein, the pioneer physicist who gave us a new understanding of the universe, claims that most of his theories did not come while he worked at that blackboard in the famous room at The Princeton Institute for Advanced Studies. They came initially in flashes of insight. They were worked out later on the blackboard in detail, but they were born in a creative vision. Louis Aggasiz is a famous pioneer biologist who has a building named for him at Harvard. He tells of an occasion when he tried to put together a key fossil fish and had to give up in frustration. Shortly afterward, he woke in the night with a complete picture of the skeleton in his mind. He went back to his laboratory and reconstructed that vision just as he had seen it.

Writers, inventors, and scientists tell us that much of their inspiration comes just before dawn. That's *when* it comes, but you and I know from *where* it comes—from God, the giver of dreams. How do we tap into those dreams and visions? The starting point is holy dissatisfaction with things as they are. We are not to settle for doing what we have always done, the way it has always been done, personally or nationally. We need to practice being receptive to new ideas. If God nudges you awake at 4:00 A.M., claim the ideas that come and write them down. Check them out in the cold light of day. If they still seem new and creative and worthwhile then proceed with that vision. But have patience; it may take seven years to prove it was genuinely a vision of God. It did for Joseph.

It is my dream that the church especially will be the fostering place for creative new ideas to bless the world. God has given His Spirit and, among other things, it is the spirit of creativity. It's been about fifty years now since two Christian men came up with a creative approach to alcoholism. Prior to the AA program, there was little hope for the hard-core alcoholic. Both medicine and psychiatry had failed to find any cure for those caught in this addiction. Two men who had suffered with the problem, Dr. Bob and Bill Wilson, got together and prayed and hammered out the twelve steps that have helped hundreds of thousands find sobriety.

How much we need a fresh approach to today's problems. We're at the threshold of a new kind of whole-person medicine. Chief Justice Warren Burger pleads for a new legal system, less costly, less time-consuming, less litigious, and above all, more just. We're finally coming to the realization that money is not the answer to better education. We need new incentives at the classroom level. Business needs to discover a system that is a four-way win, where capital, management, labor, and consumer all get a fair shake, or we will cease being an industrial nation. On a more personal scale, life in our own neighborhoods needs a creative approach. Our jobs ought to be an outlet for our creativity.

Perhaps the most pressing problem globally is to find a creative answer for the nuclear madness of our time. We have peacemakers advocating unilateral disarmament. We have peacemakers insisting that peace comes only through a strong defense. They can't both be right and perhaps the answer lies in some third approach. How much we need to find and be the creative people who can seek God's answer to the threat of nuclear holocaust. Let's bring that same God-given creativity to the world economy. There must be a way to redistribute the world's goods more equitably, especially the world's food supply. How do we begin to care for our brothers and sisters in the Third World?

Recently I was at an ecumenical healing conference in Harrisburg, Pennsylvania. At noon we had a communion service in the cathedral and Bishop Charles McNutt was presiding at the Lord's Table. After consecrating the elements, he spoke those familiar words from the Episcopal prayer book. "The gifts of God for the people of God." I believe God has gifts for His people, and the world, that none of us has as yet dreamed of. Those gifts, the byproducts of His divine friendship, will become realities as we live, more and more, in the creative dimension.

19. Love or Perish

Genesis 42–45

Everybody loves the story of Cinderella, perhaps because we identify with her. Most of us have had at least a few people along the way who made fun of us or disliked us, though they may not have been as mean as Cinderella's stepmother and ugly stepsisters. We sometimes plot revenge. "Some day I'll get even." The helpless victim longs for the time when he or she is in the driver's seat, the one in control.

My father had been a widower for many years and had several grandchildren when he married my mother. I came into the world the instant uncle of two nieces and a nephew, all much older than I. These older and smarter kids enjoyed teasing me in front of my friends. One favorite line was, "Uncle, will you give me a nickel?" I died a thousand deaths. For me, that was a reminder of the absurdity of my situation. I used to imagine that some day I'd surprise them with my dazzling success and turn their contempt into pride and admiration.

The story of Joseph is a true life version of the Cinderella story, except that in this case the ugly stepbrothers who sold Joseph into slavery come to court him and plead for a favor. What will he do? How will he behave?

I must be the only person in the world who has never seen a single episode of "Dallas," the TV soap opera. But

I happened to be in a Holiday Inn in Tennessee on the night that the public was finally told who shot J. R, and I couldn't help noticing that this was the number one topic of conversation throughout the whole hotel. In Genesis 45, we have a similar story of suspense and high drama. Joseph is now in control, and he has an opportunity to get even with his ugly stepbrothers. What's going to happen?

The Reunion

We tend to picture the God of the Old Testament as a vengeful and wrathful God, smiting unbelievers and smashing the enemies of the Israelites. But these stories in Genesis continue to strengthen the conviction I shared earlier that the God of this Old Testament book is the same God we find in the New Testament. Together, these two sections of the Bible make up the message of redemption and grace—the message which, in the New Testament, is incarnate in the person of Jesus Christ. In Joseph's reunion with his brothers he demonstrates the grace of God. He is a forerunner of Christ. He shows us what God must be like.

Jesus, at His crucifixion, prayed on behalf of His persecutors, "Father, forgive them, for they know not what they do." Joseph models that kind of an attitude. To these brothers who sold him into slavery and very nearly killed him, he says, "Do not be distressed, or angry with yourselves, because you sold me here; for God sent me before you to preserve life . . . to preserve for you a remnant on earth and to keep alive for you many survivors. So it was not you who sent me here, but God."

Over and over again, both Old and New Testaments proclaim the triumph of grace over law. Law is necessary. There are physical and scientific laws to govern the universe. We have been given moral and spiritual laws which are inexorable and if we break them, we suffer. But if we try to live by the law, we are all doomed. "All have sinned and fallen short of the glory of God." The good news of Scripture is that the grace of God is available when we break the laws. Mercy, or love, transcends justice.

How then do you and I appropriate this grace as we live day by day in the real world as God's people? Beyond that, how do we transmit that grace in our ordinary relationships to bless other people? The story of Joseph and his brethren can give us helpful. insights.

So many of the Genesis stories involve the politics of the family—the dynamics between husband and wife, parent and child, and between siblings. Over and over the same problems crop up: jealousy, favoritism, the withholding of love, the brokering of power. This is the background for the events we read about in Genesis 45. It's twenty-two years since Joseph was sold into slavery by his brothers. He is now thirty-nine years old. The whole known world at the time is gripped by famine. Joseph's father, Jacob, and his eleven brothers and their wives and children and servants are starving. They learn that food is available in Egypt, and they travel there to find help.

They do not recognize Joseph, who is in charge of disseminating the food supply, and he plays cat and mouse with them. He sets them up by concealing money in their sacks so that they are accused of stealing. The purpose of this ruse is to force them to return with their younger brother, who had been left behind because his father was unwilling to part with him. We can understand why. Rachel, Jacob's beloved wife, had just two sons, Joseph and Benjamin. Having lost Rachel and believing Joseph dead, Jacob holds Benjamin as particularly precious.

Joseph is adamant that when his family returns, they must be accompanied by their younger brother. We might wonder about his motives. I don't think he needed Benjamin as an additional hostage. I would guess his reasons were more sentimental. Benjamin is his blood brother, the only one with the same mother. I think Joseph wanted to see him. Perhaps he was also testing his brothers to determine if time and circumstances had changed them at all. Would they be as callous about Benjamin's fate as they had been about his, twenty years before? Indifferent to the effect this loss would have on their father, they had sold Joseph into slavery without a qualm.

These pathetic brothers are in a panic that Joseph plans to keep Benjamin as a permanent hostage. Reuben, the oldest one, tries to make a deal. He begs Joseph to keep him instead. If their father is deprived of his younger son, he will surely die of a broken heart. Reuben has learned something in those twenty-two years. He is willing to sacrifice himself to protect his brother. I imagine Joseph was pleased to see this kind of change.

The Cast of Characters

Let's think about the three sets of actors in this true-life biblical drama. First of all, there are the brothers. They are powerfully bound together by the memory of an unforgiven sin of the past. In addition to their initial sin against Joseph, they are partners in collusion. They have all agreed to this complicity. They have lived under a cloud for twenty-two years during which time I am sure they have lost all joy and spontaneity in their dealings with each other. They are two-dimensional, cardboard figures, flat and sad.

Second, there is the father, Jacob, the man who loved God so much he cheated to get his blessing. He calls God by the earliest name—El Shaddai, the powerful one. He keeps believing, even when his heart is breaking. In the loss of Rachel and Joseph, he grieves with his whole heart. When he receives good news, he celebrates and rejoices with his total being. Through it all, he believes and he lives in hope. He is imperfect, but he is three-dimensional and substantial. He understands God's grace.

Then, of course, there is the star of the drama, Joseph

himself. He appears cool and poised and in control as he deals with his family in this series of bizarre scenes. But from time to time, he sneaks out and moans and weeps so loudly that all of Pharaoh's household can hear him. On his brothers' first visit for grain, he overhears them speaking in their native tongue, saying that a reckoning is coming for their sins against their brother Joseph. This admission moves him to tears. He is not the controlled person he appears to be, but a man of great feeling and passion.

The Crucial Question

It's interesting to find in chapters 42, 43, and 44 that the brothers literally bow before Joseph on three separate occasions. The very dream he had related to them twenty-two years before, the one that had caused their intense hatred, was fulfilled. When Joseph finally reveals who he is, they are, of course, terrified, and rightly so. But instead of punishment, he dispenses grace. And as he asks the question which is the crucial question for all of us in all sorts of situations, "Is my father still alive?" he introduces a third dimension into their relationship. In all those situations in which we are dealing with those who have used or abused us, in major or minor ways, we need to be aware of that third dimension. If we have a living Father whom we love, how can we not respond to His other children in love?

That third dimension is inescapable for those of us who claim we are Christians. However you have sinned against me, because my Father lives, I cannot hate you. And of course our Father gives His children the grace to love. However you have sinned against me, or I against you, the crucial question is this: Is our Father still alive? Those of us who have been dealt with graciously must practice noblesse oblige.

The principle applies even on a purely secular plane. Somerset Maugham has said that the successful people in life are invariably gracious and humble and forgiving. It's the losers who are hostile, who hold grudges, and harbor resentments.

Joe Namath, the famous quarterback who played so many football games with severe injuries, once said: "When you win, nothing hurts." That must be how Joseph felt, and I'm convinced that God wants to enable us to be winners so that even when the world does its worst to us, we can say, "It doesn't hurt so much," and let go of all resentment and bitterness.

This chapter is entitled "Love or Perish," and that's our choice. It is psychologically true. If we don't love, we begin to shrivel up. We focus our lives on our hates instead of our loves. When you live by your hates, nurturing grudges, planning revenge, you undermine your psychological, spiritual, and physical health. When you live by your loves, your well-being increases. We read in the second chapter of John's first letter, verses 9, 10, and 11, "He who says he is in the light and hates his brother is in the darkness still. He who loves his brother abides in the light, and in it there is no cause for stumbling. But he who hates his brother is in the darkness and walks in the darkness, and does not know where he is going, because the darkness has blinded his eyes."

Where Love Begins

The challenge is to love or perish. And that love ought to begin with ourselves. Grace must be appropriated there if we are going to be channels of grace to others. Joseph must have been subject to bouts of self-hate in those long years in Egypt. We can imagine him thinking, "If only I had been less arrogant, more loving, more relational, more sensitive to my brothers and their feelings. If I had behaved differently, I wouldn't be here in this strange land." At some point along the way, he must have made peace with all those past mistakes and said, "It doesn't matter. God meant it for good. I'm here by His choice. I can forgive myself and move on." We lay hold on grace when we can begin to experience that kind of self-love.

Monday is my study day, the day in which I polish and

finish my sermon for the coming Sunday. One Monday night, I went to bed at a reasonable hour, only to wake up at 3:45 in the morning, unable to go back to sleep. The week ahead looked like a disaster. It was overscheduled. We were short of staff. There were unexpected problems, and I knew I could not be in all of the places I needed to be, or where God wanted me to be. It was going to be a mess. From 3:45 to 6:00 A.M. I lay there trying to juggle and rearrange all the commitments of the next four days. Then it seemed as though the Lord finally spoke to me. "What were you working on yesterday?" "A great sermon," I said. "It was all about the fact that You are in everything and able to work for good in whatever happens to us." "Do you believe that in the mess you're in right now?" the Lord seemed to say. I said, "Yes, I do," and I fell sound asleep. The alarm went off at 6:15, but I had fifteen minutes of deep and dreamless sleep.

Dealing with Enemies

Second, this love or perish ultimatum concerns your enemies. In the prayer Jesus taught His disciples, one phrase is, "Forgive us our debts as we forgive our debtors." That advice is not for the sake of our debtors, but for our own peace of mind. Forgiving our debtors doesn't make us spiritual giants; it is a means to survival. The disciples asked the Lord, "How many times must I forgive? Is seven times enough?" "Seventy times seven" was His answer, and I don't think that meant 490 times, but an infinite number of times. The motives of the person seeking forgiveness are unimportant. Whether or not that person is sincere or deserving—forgive, forgive, forgive, for your own sake. It is a discipline that will help us understand something of the sovereignty of God, that for His own best plans God is using even those people who do not wish us well and do not want us to succeed.

When I worked in New York City, I got to know J. C. Penney, the famous storekeeper, during his last years. He credits his success to his conviction that his critics were actually valuable friends. "I thank God for those people who come in and tell me what's wrong with my business and suggest ways to improve it," he told me. He built a whole chain of stores using the suggestions of dissatisfied customers. He applied this love or perish principle to his business philosophy.

Last year I talked to a doctor who has a wholistic approach to life and medicine. He said, "I had an interesting case a while ago. One of my old patients developed rheumatoid arthritis very suddenly. Her hands were seriously affected. After the examination, we sat down in my office to talk. I asked what had been happening to her." (That's not a bad approach when someone has a sudden physical problem.) "She said, 'Doctor, I know what you're getting at. I know exactly when this condition started and, furthermore, I have no intention of forgiving him.' She never revealed who that was, but she's still suffering and I can't do much for her." I don't believe in a direct cause-and-effect connection between resentment and illness, but we are forced to conclude that there is some connection. That's why the Lord who loves us insists that we forgive. He wants us to survive.

Joseph's statements to his brothers underscore that while they meant what they did for evil, God meant it for good. We don't know how that works. We all have free will and, in this case, the brothers chose to do what they did—to plot to murder their brother, and then sell him to a passing caravan. Joseph does not minimize their sin, but the primary issue is that God worked His purposes through them to put Joseph in a place to save their lives and the lives of many. Love or perish is the ultimatum for us nationally and internationally. The wounds of the Civil War are still visible because the Union was unwilling to love and forgive. Had Lincoln not been assassinated, the story might have been different. It was his intention to embrace the conquered states and demand no retribution.

Joseph chose to love in spite of his feelings of anger, grief, or sorrow. Before he revealed his identity to his family, we read that he wept aloud on three different occasions. Joseph, like his father Jacob, was a man of strong feelings and he let them show.

Dealing with Feelings

Perhaps we should say a word here about dealing with our feelings. It seems to me we have four choices. First of all, we can strive to have none. The goal of some Eastern religions is to seek to feel nothing, to attain a state of Nirvana in which nothing moves you. Assuming that could be achieved, it could only be done at the expense of our humanity. God made us in His image, with passions and feelings. To strive to have no feelings is a kind of death wish.

Second, we can repress or deny our feelings. We can say, "I don't really feel this way." A great many conservative Christians live this way because they think feelings in themselves are bad or immoral. But we are judged by our actions, not our feelings. We can't control our feelings—feelings of anger or grief or joy—but we don't need to act on negative feelings. Denying our negative feelings, we begin to block out all the good and positive feelings that enrich our lives.

The third option is to be controlled by our feelings, to do whatever feels good. That was the motto of the Me Generation of the seventies. At best, it's an immature attitude and at worst, dangerous and destructive.

Finally, we can let our feelings out, as Joseph did frequently, and as his father did. Joseph wept, and he acted in faith and love because he was not a prisoner of his feelings. Small Christian groups can provide the climate in which we can get our feelings out. We can confess our anger toward our children or our boss or our parents. The group is the place where we can weep, share our anguish, and claim healing through prayer. I was told about a couple who were asked the secret of their successful marriage. It seems they agreed on their wedding day never to go to bed angry.

"Sometimes we haven't slept for three days," they confessed, "but we've kept that vow."

Coval B. McDonald, writing in a recent issue of *The Journal for the Scientific Study of Religion,* claims that the joyous exuberance of religiously conservative Protestants at worship and their ready smiles may actually mask a tendency toward depressive moods. In diagnoses of 7050 patients at a Midwestern psychiatric clinic, depression showed up significantly only among Protestants who typically belonged to evangelical and Pentecostal churches. He says, "Repetitive joy of the Lord and praise of the Lord might be attempts at controlling depression." McDonald is himself a United Presbyterian minister and former pastor. By way of contrast, the biblical patriarchs, like Joseph and Jacob, felt free to express their feelings. They were those who could rage and weep, celebrate and praise.

Joseph's brothers hated him enough to sell him into slavery. Few of us have such deadly enemies, but for all of us, there are those people who will not celebrate when we succeed and who will secretly rejoice when we fail. Is it normal to feel negative about them? Of course! It's not pleasant to have enemies. But must we love them? Yes. If not, we perish. Remember, loving is not the same as liking. Loving requires seeing the other person as a child of God and wanting His best for that person.

In this moving dialogue depicting Joseph's reconciliation with his brothers, we find the secret. However hatefully your enemy is behaving right now—the enemy in your bed, your home, your office, your school, or your church—consider that person and ask yourself the pivotal question, "Is my Father still alive?" We cannot call God Father and hate one of His children. God demands that we love our enemies, but He also makes that possible. He gives us a new spirit if we ask Him for it. Furthermore, if we believe in God's sovereignty, then we know our God is big enough to use all of the circumstances of our lives, even our enemies, to put us where He intends us to be.

20. A Friend for Now and a Friend Forever

Genesis 48–50

As we come to the end of this journey through Genesis, let's review some of the cornerstones of understanding that have been repeated over and over again in this part of God's Word. First of all, we see that the God of Genesis is the same God we find in the person of Jesus Christ. Jesus said, "If you have seen me, you have seen the Father." Jesus and the Father, Creator, God of Genesis, are one, one who wills good things for us and offers us His friendship and a personal relationship. Second, grace inevitably transcends the law. God made a universe of moral, spiritual, and physical laws, but He has made provision for the fact that we will all inevitably break those laws. We are a forgiven people. God's grace is sufficient.

Another central purpose of God's Word here and throughout the Bible is to point up the difference between faith and unbelief. Faith is trusting in a God who is bigger than our unfaith and our unbelief. Our faith is in God, and not in ourselves, our own goodness or our strength. We find this message as we read about all the old patriarchs of Genesis, and particularly in the story of Joseph.

Finally, Genesis is an ode to the sovereignty of God. The theme is nowhere more poignantly or beautifully discerned than in the last chapter of Genesis. Jacob is now dead, and the brothers suspect this turn of events will bring unpleasant changes. To put it in the vernacular, they say to Joseph, "Our father is dead. There is no longer any reason to keep us alive now. We will surely get the punishment we deserve for our betrayal." Joseph continues to believe that God was in all that happened. He used their hatred and cruelty to bring about His will. Joseph continues to forgive his brothers, his enemies.

Accepting Reality

But the final enemy for all of us is death. These last chapters in Genesis describe two deaths, Jacob's and Joseph's. The Bible always describes death realistically, not with the euphemisms we have grown so accustomed to. We have all seen cards for departed loved ones with those chirpy messages like, "He is not dead, he is just away." The Bible does not resort to such subterfuge. Death is a reality, the inevitable end for all living things.

For most of our culture, death is the ultimate fear and we seek to camouflage that fear. One of my favorite theologians, Woody Allen, has said, "I'm not afraid of dying. I just don't want to be there when it happens." But joking about it is like whistling in the dark or spitting in the wind. I once heard Carlyle Marney say, "God means to kill us all."

There is a strange dichotomy here—we have not lived fully until we have come to terms with our own death. Conversely, we are not prepared for death until we have learned to live. Death and life are inextricably bound together. Those who have found meaning and purpose and fulfillment in life are more reconciled to death and those who have come to grips with their eventual death have begun to find meaning and purpose and fulfillment in life. I read somewhere, "If at first you do succeed, try, try not to be insufferable." None of us will get a second chance at dying. We don't have the luxury of saying, "I learned a lot the first time. I'll do it better the next time." We have only one chance to die, and God doesn't want us to blow it. He wants us to do it with grace and dignity and with a resolute hope in His ultimate purpose for us.

Making Preparations

In preparing for death, Jacob had a good deal of business to conduct with his twelve sons, each in a different way. To Joseph he bequeathed the side of a mountain, and he blessed Joseph's two sons. There was no single, all-inclusive blessing. Rather, Joseph dealt with each of his children individually. We read that when all of the business of living was done, he drew up his feet into the bed and breathed his last and was gathered to his people. He had already made detailed plans for his burial. He didn't leave that important matter to his children. They had deceived him too many times before.

We would do well to follow Jacob's example. I heard about a prominent local doctor in Abingdon, Virginia, who arranged to have his tombstone carved before he died so it would be done correctly. It gives his name, Dr. David Kinsolving, and the month and date of his birth, but not the year. And then these words: "I am here and gone. I had a good time." Dr. Kinsolving knew exactly what message he wished to convey to future generations. He didn't leave that selection to his widow or children.

Jacob planned for his death with care. As we said, he had a personal word for each of his children. He scourged three of them, warned some others, and blessed the rest, particularly Judah and Joseph. He had words of prophecy about each one, and also about Joseph's two sons. Then he died. He died without the hope of resurrection, because that revelation from God came much later.

Nevertheless, he died trusting the God of Abraham and Isaac and the God of the generations to come. He saw life as a process and covenant. Having come to Egypt with his sons because of the famine, he was honored there by Pharaoh even in death. He was embalmed, a practice reserved for royalty, and given a state funeral. But in spite of knowing such honor would be his, he had been determined not to be buried in Egypt. All the honor given him by the most powerful nation in the world was inconsequential compared to the covenant he had made with God. It was the same covenant entered into by his grandfather Abraham and his father Isaac, and it is the covenant you and I have as believers. Powerful empires come and go, yet God's covenants and purposes are eternal.

Jacob had been adamant. "Don't bury me in Egypt. Bury me back in that little cave Abraham purchased from the Hittites when Sarah died." That's the land where God had made promises to Jacob and his ancestors for all the generations yet to come. Jacob had the long view of life. His faithfulness was the means of blessing God's people in all the ensuing centuries, generations of men and women he would never see.

Running the Race

I have done a good many day-long workshops in churches around the country, and often I'll ask the participants to draw a line illustrating how long they think they will live. I suspect that many of us will live about as long as we expect to live. Barring unforeseen accidents, death can be a self-fulfilling prophecy. This exercise usually turns up some people who predict they are going to live to be one hundred, and I don't think that's an unreasonable hope. Others say forty, or fifty, or seventy. We all know how much our lives are shaped by our expectations. It seems to me we can have at least three different kinds of expectations as we view our lives.

1. We may see our life as a hundred-yard dash. We say, "Who knows how long I'll live? I'd better run as fast as I can. I'm going to grab all the gusto there is because I have

no idea how soon it will all be over." We work too hard, we play too hard. Our lives are full of frenetic activity.

2. Perhaps we see life as a marathon, somewhat like the Boston Marathon. "If I can just finish, I don't even care about winning. I'm just hoping to hang on long enough to make it to the end." Life may be grueling and wearisome, and we are hoping we will have enough strength and energy to get through it.

3. We can see life as a relay race, as Jacob did. At baptism, we are brought to the altar and, symbolically speaking, are given a baton, one to pass on through many generations. As we grab it, we start our own covenant with God, and as we grow into adulthood, we run the race of faith. When we die, we have a sense of passing the baton on, an awareness of being a part of God's drama. Life doesn't end with us. It begins and ends with God. That was Jacob's understanding, and he prepared to die with care and we need to do so as well. Take time to make all the important decisions well in advance.

Planning Ahead

Begin by planning what you want done with your remains. Buy a gravesite, or a tomb, perhaps your own special Cave of Machpelah, and indicate what you want in the way of a tombstone and what you'd like carved on it. If you want cremation, leave instructions about that. I had a call just recently from a delightful saint who is a member of our congregation. She wanted to know what I thought about cremation. And then she had one further question. "Would it be morbid if I wrote a letter to be read at the memorial service?" I told her it was a wonderful idea. What a blessing a word from her will be to those who are grieving over their loss. There's nothing morbid about that.

Last year our missions pastor, Tim Dearborn, went to Africa for three weeks, leaving his wife and three daughters behind.

He left with them a whole stack of letters, one to each of those four girls for each day of his absence. In other words, each one got twenty-one letters. Now that takes some doing. His family claims it was the shortest three-week trip Daddy ever took. Sometimes the children's letters contained bubble gum or balloons. Hearing about that loving act made me sad that I had never thought of doing something like that. I was away from home a lot when my children were young, and how I wish I had been that thoughtful. I blew it, but it's not too late for any of us to do the thoughtful thing in terms of our funerals. We can leave a message behind and share the deepest things of our heart with our loved ones.

A while back I read about a legal firm opening new offices in Baltimore. Unfortunately, the florist got the order confused and sent a spray to the law firm that said, "Deepest sympathy." That was not as unfortunate as the message that accompanied the flowers delivered to the funeral home: "Congratulations on your new location." We're all going to have a new location one day. Expect it and make detailed plans and your heirs will bless you.

Unfinished Business

Leave nothing undone. Tell those you love how you feel about them. Take care of all that unfinished business. If there's some place you want to visit, some work you want to start, a cause you want to invest in, do it. Do the things that God has put into your heart. Don't delay. Don't die with regrets and unfulfilled desires if you can help it.

Recently I read about a lady in a community near Seattle who is now eighty-four and involved in many causes. She's been driving the same car for nineteen years and she had vowed that when the car stopped running, she was going to give up and die. One day the engine belched black smoke and the old car expired. There was no way to resurrect it. There and then she broke her vow. She bought a secondhand reconditioned engine and the nineteen-year-old car is still running and she is still running. Here's what she told the *Seattle Times* reporter.

> As the cells in my body renew
> And my purpose in life I review,
> I find growing older, I'm now growing bolder
> And increasingly hard to subdue.

I commend that to you. One day God will call this spunky lady home, but in the meantime, she's full of life.

What exactly is a full life? We know eagles and swans can live to be one hundred, and carp and pike to one hundred and fifty. They can hardly be said to enjoy a full life. Lots of years are not synonymous with a full life. A full life is one in which you do everything you and God intended for you to do in the time that you have.

Get rid of your resentments. Forgive everybody you've been nursing a grudge against, all the people who have, by omission or commission, wronged you. If anybody ever had justifiable cause for resentment, Joseph did. Instead, he forgave his brothers and claimed the sovereignty of God over his life. We are all going to die. We hope to be forgiven as we have forgiven those who trespass against us. I am reminded of the poor woman who was ordering a tombstone for her recently deceased husband. She asked for something simple: "Just carve his name and put on there, 'To my husband' in a suitable place." To her consternation, the final product read, "To my husband in a suitable place." This judgment about her spouse was unintentional, but one way to prepare to die is to have no grudges and to be able to forgive your enemies.

Use your material possessions to bless your heirs, your friends, your companions, your church, and the causes you care about. A member of our congregation works in the church office for a typically modest salary, and she told me recently that she plans to leave 10 percent of her estate to her church. She has several children, but she is determined to say something in death about her commitment to Christ and His Kingdom. Some time ago, I read about a ninety-year-old man who, while still living, gave his entire life's savings to his little college in West Virginia. "I want you to know that ordinary people like me are grateful for the education we got in your school," he wrote, and he sent them fifty thousand dollars. He's a model for all of us. If God has blessed you with more than you will require to live out your years, don't leave it all behind. Be selfish enough to give it away now and to have the fun and joy of seeing it bless others.

Finally, trust God with your future. Trust God with your old age. Old age in our culture is not a blessing. The biblical patriarchs like Jacob were venerated in their old age. Both old age and death are gifts. God means to bless us in both. A friend wrote me about a ninety-five-year-old Latin teacher, a Vassar graduate, who lives in Connecticut and is a member of his congregation. Every morning she reads the *New York Times* and *Christian Science Monitor.* Then she proceeds to work on a research paper dealing with trends in educational philosophy, and she is also studying computer languages. This very old lady is in her full powers, and I think that's what God intends for most of us. Live to the hilt. Live all the life God has for you. When death comes, you can say, "Welcome, friend. I can't wait to see what's beyond the veil."

An eighty-six-year-old friend sent me this poem:

You tell me I am growing old, but that's not really so,
The house I live in may be worn, and that of course I know.
It's been in use a good long time and weathered many a
  gale.
I'm therefore not surprised to find it's getting somewhat frail.

You tell me I'm getting old, you mix my house with me,
You're looking at the outside, that's all that most folks see.
The dweller in the little house is young and bright and gay
Just starting out a life that lasts through long eternal day.

These few short years can't make me old, I feel I'm in my
   youth.
Eternity lies just ahead, full of life and joy and truth.
We will not fret to see the house grow shabby day by day,
But look ahead to our new home, which never will decay.

My house is getting ready in the land beyond the sky,
Its architect and builder is my Saviour now on high.

Endings and Beginnings

Genesis is the book of beginnings—the beginning of the
world and of the human race and of the pilgrimage of those
who are called to be God's people. The book of beginnings,
rightly, ends in death as it must. God has so designed life
that all beginnings have endings, and death is the inevitable
end of all life.

But you know, death may be very much like birth. Think
about a fetus in a mother's womb. Every need is supplied.
There is protection from the cold and heat. All necessary
nutriments are provided. What fetus would choose to come
into the world? They arrive kicking and screaming, and I
don't blame them. Life is not as comfortable or trouble-free
as the womb, but it's more exciting.

In the same sense, maybe death looks so frightening because we can't see what happens on the other side. But we
catch a glimpse from our Lord Himself, who promised His
disciples, "I go to prepare a place for you." I like to think
it's a place where, among other pursuits, we can worship
God as our Creator and enjoy His friendship for eternity.

About the author:

Bruce Larson is Senior Pastor of University Presbyterian Church in Seattle, Washington, a call that he answered in 1980. Prior to that time he was involved in church renewal ministry as President of Faith at Work, and he has also been a Visiting Fellow at Princeton Theological Seminary. This is his nineteenth book. He has over two million copies of his books in print, all of them showing how biblical faith is concerned with life and relationships rather than abstract doctrines. His most recent writings include *Wind and Fire: Living Out the Book of Acts, There's a Lot More to Health Than Not Being Sick,* and *Luke* (vol. 3 of *The Communicator's Commentary* series).